ALL WE NEED IS

LOVE

Sadly something not all my brothers and sisters received

Daisy May Sewell

Pen Press

© Ron Sewell 2011

All rights reserved

First published in Great Britain by Pen Press

All paper used in the printing of this book has been made from
wood grown in managed, sustainable forests.

ISBN13: 978-1-78003-115-6

Printed and bound in the UK
Pen Press is an imprint of
Indepenpress Publishing Limited
25 Eastern Place
Brighton
BN2 1GJ

A catalogue record of this book is available from
the British Library

Cover design by Jacqueline Abromeit

Daisy May Sewell

Sadly Daisy died before her book was published. A few of the tributes paid to her posthumously are shown below:

'Daisy was wonderful PR for dogs. She was beautiful, elegant, had impeccable manners and was the life and soul of every beach party.'
Emer Joyce, solicitor and friend in Co. Clifdon, Connemara.

'She never missed a meeting of the board. She greeted all the directors as they arrived. Her quizzical "looks" with those communicative eyes played a real part in preserving harmony. Daisy lived respected and died regretted.'
Dr Terence R Keen, friend, and former CEO of South Devon College.

'I have known Ron for four decades. His dogs were always well trained and well mannered, but Daisy took the biscuit. Whenever she visited our home, or joined us in a pub outing, she reminded me of that old Victorian adage; dogs should be seen and not heard. She would lie down and become virtually invisible until it was time to leave, whereupon she would give us a friendly lick by way of farewell.'
Peter Nathan, friend.

'There has never been a dog like her and never will be. She was very special with a gentle, wonderful nature. Everyone who knew her, loved her; particularly our dog, Wrinkles, who she adored.'
Sally Stallard, owner of her friend, Wrinkles.

This book is dedicated to my sister, Hopeless,
who was 'put to sleep' (killed) when she was
seven months old.

Her owner made the mistake of taking her to
an out-of-date trainer who believed in coercion,
and a self-appointed 'expert' (her owner's
brother) who bullied his sister into believing
that Hopeless *had* to be killed.

Every dog that has ever followed its master or mistress
gives an immeasurable sum of love and fidelity. Sadly,
many owners are unable or unwilling to reciprocate.

Introduction by Clarissa Baldwin of Dogs Trust

It is an honour to have been invited to say a few words about *All we need is love* and to have been given the opportunity to write about the work of Dogs Trust.

To my mind it is often quite acceptable to be anthropomorphic, in fact, I defy anyone who has a companion animal to say that they don't talk to their pet. What is more – I am sure we all agree that our pets know exactly what we are saying too! In Daisy May Sewell's book, *All we need is love*, we see a very fine example of a dog in human clothing. You only have to read the accolades from those who knew Daisy well to know that Ron and she had a close and loving friendship.

At Dogs Trust we believe in celebrating the very special and unique bond that humans have with dogs. The understanding that can develop between a dog and his owner is one of the great joys of life. In this enchanting book we see a lovely description of this bond, so well written by one of our four-legged friends.

Dogs Trust (formerly known as the National Canine Defence League) was founded in 1891. After a somewhat chequered history, one that left us with some triumphant battles won but very little cash to carry on, we were reformed in the early 1970s and our non-destruction policy made sacrosanct. It was then that the fight to save and improve the lives of dogs throughout the United Kingdom really started.

Today we operate 17 Rehoming Centres and if you have ever visited any of them, I hope you would agree that the facilities and our care for the dogs is second to none. We look after around 16,000 dogs a year and ensure that our policy of never putting a healthy dog to sleep is at the heart of everything we do. The majority of the dogs in our care are able to be rehomed fairly quickly but some have had the misfortune to be owned by irresponsible owners who have not taken the time to train or socialise their pets. Without early socialisation and basic training, some dogs can be harder to rehome as they may have learned bad habits and require a very specialised home. This is where our Training and Behaviour Advisers step in and set about making these dogs acceptable companions for people wanting to rehome a rescue dog.

The Rehoming Centres are the shop windows of our work and we are extremely blessed with having dedicated staff to care for, train and find suitable homes for unwanted dogs. But we didn't just want our work to be classed as a 'soup kitchen' solution – we really wanted to do something to stop the deaths of so many thousands of dogs who ended up being euthanased for want of a good home. So in 2000 we launched our neutering campaigns where, in certain areas of the UK, we encourage and pay for a substantial amount of the cost of the operation. It is positive that from when statistics first began, the UK has reduced its destruction rate from 40,000 dogs per year to under 7,000 in 2008. We like to think that the Dogs Trust neutering campaigns have played a significant part in this reduction but we are not complacent and are well aware that a lot more needs to be done.

Education also plays a large part in our work; eight education officers go into schools, youth groups and communities to pass on the messages of responsible dog ownership to the dog owners of tomorrow. We know that these children act as voice pieces for Dogs Trust by communicating what they've learned to their parents and siblings. Of course, legislation also plays a large part in our work. We were pleased when the Animal Welfare Act eventually reached the Statute Book in 2006 but we will be even happier when Secondary Regulations to control greyhound breeding and racing, prevent puppy farms and control pet vending, to name but a few, are introduced. We are working hard to make this happen as quickly as possible.

I could go on forever on my soap box but suffice to say, please visit one of our centres; if you know anyone who wants a dog, please point them in our direction or visit www.dogstrust.org.uk for further information.

As I finish reading Daisy's book, I feel there are some really important messages, some enchanting moments coupled with stories of great sadness. There are two very famous quotes which, for me, describe the special relationship between man and dog:

'In life the firmest friend, the first to welcome, foremost to defend.' *George Gordon, Lord Byron*; and,

'No matter how little money and how few possessions you own, having a dog makes you rich.' *Louis Sabin*; and of course,

'A dog is for life, not just for Christmas,' the slogan of Dogs Trust.

Clarissa Baldwin
Dogs Trust

My Brothers and Sisters

Patch

Hopeless

Pinky

Nosey

The Bully (Pete)

Happy

Clever Clogs

The Boss

Contents

PART ONE

Chapter One

Puppyhood

My first memories are similar to those I have in the morning when, snug in the warmth which has developed in my bed, I am still half asleep though conscious of my environment.

Similarly, my first feelings as a young, blind pup were of the warmth and comfort of resting against my mother's body, surrounded by other warm bodies. Our collective feeling of comfort was enhanced when we were able to snuffle our way along the scent which guided us to a teat to draw the deliciously warm, creamy milk from one of our mother's nipples. These were moments of pure bliss. Unfortunately, there was not always one available. As we grew older and gained our sight, we realised that there were nine of us puppies, while Mum only had eight teats! Hence, there were frequent bouts of pushing and shoving as the pup without tried to secure one.

Once, a particularly desperate push for a spare teat resulted in me being heaved out of the litter. It was a moment of pure panic to lose physical contact with my family. I swung my heavy head; my eyes were not yet open, from side to side, desperately trying to regain contact. It was a great relief when a set of unseen teeth gently lifted me back into the fray.

Brothers and sisters

As our eyes cleared, and we began to see, to recognise brothers and sisters, we needed less sleep and started to play with each other. Our games were really mock fights. Our tussles helped to establish our pecking order in the litter. We tumbled over and under each other, seeking to gain a dominant position with our young milk teeth at the throat of an upturned rival who was then expected to submit. This was the objective, but sometimes I would find myself upturned at the mercy of a bigger brother and I would have to be the one who submitted. As I was to realise later, it is very important for we dogs to be able to establish our place in the pecking order of dominance or submission.

Our youngest sister, who had been the last to be born, always lost out in these games – I heard the humans calling her a runt, meaning that she was the weakest of the litter, less able to fight for her share of the food and therefore not as well nourished. In fact, we realised that it was her plaintiff squeals of desperation which had been the backdrop to our own search for a teat.

As I grew older and began think about things for myself, I sometimes wondered why our mother did not try to help her, though I got the impression that a human hand would come down from time to time to help her onto a teat. Years later I met a very wise old dog who told me that it was nature's way of ensuring that only fit puppies survived. So humans' interference resulted in puppies unable to cope, physically or temperamentally, with life.

Our mother

As we moved from being pups into being puppies, we began to realise that both the nipples and the long, wet, red tongue which had periodically appeared to wash us, belonged to our mother, a beautiful tri-colour collie bitch with lovely eyes that sparkled with love if we were good, but looked hard and frosty when we weren't! One glance from these steely eyes was all that we needed by way of discipline.

Our home was a boxed-off section of a cowshed, which gave us plenty of room to fight and tumble and to chase each other around, while a dividing wall enabled our mother to jump up out of the way for a rest whenever we got too much for her.

Brothers and sisters

As our games continued, not only did we evolve our 'pecking order' but our differing personalities became more evident, so each of us gained our own identity. Let me just describe my brothers and sisters to you within this pecking order:

The Boss established himself not so much by his physical strength, but by his personality. He simply oozed confidence. Though only a pup, he showed signs of developing into a magnificent adult, with the traditional collie colouring.

The Bully owed his position purely to physical strength, which he delighted in using quite unnecessarily so, while the rest of us had to give way; we did not like him.

Happy was a gorgeous young female who was always so happy, her tail never stopped wagging. She seemed to regard life as one tremendous joke, so her face always seemed to be alight with laughter. She had the traditional collie colouring, but her fur was finer and shorter than usual.

Clever Clogs was actually my twin sister in that we had a tan-coloured undercoat which showed through on our faces, and hind legs. She was the cleverest of us. If there was a way of opening the door to our pen, or creating an opening in the fencing, she would be the one to do it. She was the ringleader in all the exploits which got us into trouble.

Tiptoes is me. I was in the middle of the pecking order at number five, being neither over aggressive or unduly submissive. I heard humans describing me as a tri-colour, in that, like my sister, I had black, white, and tan colouring, but shorter and finer fur than usual. Apparently my brothers and sisters thought of me as Tiptoes – I heard humans describing me as 'highly strung'. I always seemed to be charged with a nervous energy which kept me dancing on my toes.

Nosey was just plain Nosey. His nose always seemed to be well in front of his body, to be seeking out new smells, new activities, new visitors. He was a very gentle, likeable brother with whom I got on best. Though he ranked sixth in the pecking order, it was not so much that he was soft, but merely that he was too preoccupied because he had a hidden strength to his personality.

Pinky and Patch were described by their distinguishing features, a pink patch on Pinky's nose, and a black patch over Patch's eye, because they had no real personalities. They always submitted. They never even attempted to be dominant. In fact, they were pleasant enough, but colourless males.

Hopeless, the runt of the litter, was hopeless! She was born below par, and her lack of size meant that she did not get her full quota of milk from our mother. She was the 'punch bag' of the litter. If some of the junior members got fed up with having to submit to its leaders, they took it out on Hopeless because they could at least have the satisfaction of dominating her.

Initially we were in our own cocoon focussed on our mother, particularly her teats, and each other. Almost overnight, our horizons widened. We became more aware of our pen, and the cowshed of which it formed a part. Sometimes there were frightening noises from tractors and farm machinery. Above all, there were humans!

Helen!

While fighting for our teats, we had been aware of hands appearing and disappearing. Now we saw them connected to 'our' human. She was called Helen and, to us, seemed a real giant. What captivated us was her gentleness, and her empathy. She understood how we felt, but above all, we were all captivated by her smile which extended to her eyes. In fact, it seemed to pervade her being. We all fell head over heels in love! She would spend most of the day with us, keeping us company, giving each of us a cuddle, playing with us, and calming us down when we were frightened by the noises from the farmyard. If only we had been able to stay in that blissful state of happiness.

Visitors

Progressively, we started to get more and more visitors. All sorts and sizes of humans came to see us, pick us up, cuddle and play with us. We enjoyed it best when children from the village stopped by. When they crouched down to play with us, they were far less frightening, and they taught us new games. My favourite was playing tug of war with a piece of sacking, or trying to jump up when it was dangled above my head.

Toys

Once, Helen brought down a selection of toys for us to play with. But, as we tried to bite them, they squeaked. Hopeless shot into the far corner of the pen and stayed there shivering with fright. Happy fell about laughing as we all sat back on our haunches with surprise. Clever Clogs, as usual, was the one who figured out that if she gave a sharp bite in the middle of the toy, it squeaked. Once she figured out what we had to do, we had a great time and created so much noise that Helen would only let us have them for short periods at a time.

Hopeless always kept as far away as possible whenever we played with these toys. The Bully, as usual, used his strength to make sure he always had first go with a toy and made sure that nobody could take it from him once he had it. The Boss joined in but – as with all our other games – did not get too het up or possessive. Pinky and Patch skittered around us as we played. They seldom got a chance to squeak the squeakers. Initially, our mother seemed very happy to watch us play with the humans who visited us; particularly the children. Whenever Helen picked us up, our mother would snuggle up to her; give the pup she was holding a lick, and then give Helen a quick lick as if she was sharing Helen's joy. Equally when the village children came to play, our mother would leave them to it with a contented smile on her face.

Playing fair

We puppies had to learn to react with other dogs. If, when we bit one of our brothers or sisters, they yelped with pain, we realised that we had bitten them too hard. Equally, if one of them bit me too hard, I knew what it felt like.

So, if we were getting the worst of the game, we learned how to submit. Equally, if we were winning with our game, we had to learn to accept their submission. We had to learn how to play fair with each other and thus build relationships.

Normally, our mother had not interfered but as she got more involved; her eyes would drill into us, and she would give a soft growl. She altered her approach to us. Rather than 'nursing' us, she showed her dominance and required us to be subservient to her.

My world changed

Then, my world was changed forever, everything changed. My mother changed. When humans came, she became edgy and anxious. She would patrol up and down the wall of the pen anxiously. Sometimes, she would jump down and try to get between the pup and the people. Once, she even tried to pull The Bully out of the hands of a male human. As innocent pups, we could not understand what was the matter with her.

Then, to our horror, these new humans started taking different puppies away with them. Our mother tried to explain that just as she belonged to Helen, so each of us pups had to belong to another human. She hoped that our new owners would be as good to us as Helen was to her. We were too young to understand, but some of her tension rubbed off on us. The Boss retained his self-confidence. Happy was sure it would work out. Nosey remained Nosey. Clever Clogs and I could not really restrain ourselves enough to be anxious, but Pinky and Patch became reluctant to be held by these strange, questioning hands. Hopeless did her best to avoid being caught.

A confusing outing

My interest was aroused when a very attractive lady came to play with us. She tried to play with each of us in turn, and even did her best to entice Hopeless into being fondled. Since most of the human visitors couldn't be bothered with Hopeless, I thought that this was very kind of her. I heard her tell Helen that she felt sorry for her. She left, but came back with quite a kind-looking but disconcerting man who did not get involved in the fondling, but merely stood back watching us.

They left, but came back a few days later, loaded The Boss, Hopeless, and I, into a wicker basket and drove away with us in their car. All of us were so worried about being shut in a basket, and the movement of the car, that we did not have time to worry about what was happening to us.

Eventually we arrived at their house, and were taken into their garden to play. This was fun. We did not realise it, but they were trying to make up their minds which of us to choose. I think the man was taken by The Boss; the woman felt sorry for Hopeless, but most of the friends who were called in to meet us seemed to be going for me. One friend, a nice lady called Milly, seemed to be particularly keen that they chose me. The couple seemed to be so kind and understanding, I tried to keep my paws crossed that they would choose me. When we drove back to the farm, the woman cuddled all three of us in her lap. From what I could gather from their conversation, the man was saying that Hopeless was – sadly – hopeless, and since their son's dog, Hamlet, would be coming to stay with them, they ought to choose me. My chest swelled with pride but I was confused to be taken back to Helen. What was happening?

The Boss

The Boss was the first to go. It turned out that one of the men we had thought to be a farm worker was a neighbouring farmer who had a large flock of sheep. The Boss was very proud that he had been chosen to be a real sheep dog. He went off very happily to learn how to manage sheep on behalf of his owner. Our mother seemed very happy and proud that he had been chosen. It meant that she would be able to keep her eye on him as he worked in the adjoining fields.

His early departure changed our lives. Whether we liked it or not, we were going to have to leave our snug little world and belong to another human or a family of humans. We became steadily more anxious as another brother or sister left us; particularly when we saw our beloved Helen wiping the tears away from her eyes as another puppy went.

Nosey

Nosey was the next to go. He went with what seemed to be a very nice couple of elderly humans. True to form, he was so busy nosing them and their car that he did not spare us, or his mother, or even Helen, a backward glance.

Happy

Happy went off soon afterwards, to a young, married couple, who said that they wanted a dog because they were not able to have children. Our mother circled around Helen trying to voice her disquiet, asking, 'What will happen if they do have children?' but we were too young to understand the question, let alone give an answer.

The Bully

Our mother was even more worried by a man who came several times to look at The Bully. Though Helen seemed impressed by his clothes and polite manners, my mother told us that she sensed a hidden anger within him. In fact she said he was 'evil'. We didn't know what that meant. It sounded bad. On his first visit, as he was holding The Bully in his hand, our mother tried to take him away from the man. Each time he came, our mother circled anxiously. Humans don't seem to be able to pick up the vibes in the same way we dogs do, so off The Bully went. Cocky to the end, he thought he would be able to stand up for himself. How wrong he was, as he was to discover to his cost.

Clever Clogs

In the melee of all the people coming and going, one lady stood out for her self-confidence. Like the couple who had taken me home, she seemed to have an instinctive empathy with my brothers, sisters and I. She quickly singled out my sister Clever Clogs and asked if she could take her away to a nearby empty barn. We were intrigued. What was going to happen? When Clever Clogs came back, she said how impressed she was by the woman's attempts to get to know her better. She had played several games with her to see how quickly she had reacted. Clever Clogs was most impressed by the time and trouble taken to get to know and understand her, just as I had been impressed by the lady and gentleman who had taken me away with them in the car, and to their home. My sister was sad to leave me, and Helen, but thrilled that she seemed to be going with a lady who had shown so much empathy.

Pinky

Several families had come with children pleading with their parents to be allowed to have a puppy as their Christmas present. Helen was very good. She pointed out that a puppy should be for life, not just for Christmas, and managed to persuade several pairs of parents to leave empty handed; often with children in tears. Eventually Pinky went off with what seemed to be an elderly couple, who seemed nice enough but without any experience of owning a dog.

Patch

Another family came with a young, petulant, spoiled son, who had a very much nicer, older sister. We hated being fondled by him since he would surreptitiously pinch us. Again, our mother tried to show Helen how anxious she was, but since several people had called at the same time, Helen was not able to concentrate on what was going on, and so Patch disappeared. As he looked back at me I saw a worried look spread over his face.

Finally, Hopeless

This left me and Hopeless. I couldn't understand why anybody in their right minds would choose such a pathetic creature as Hopeless, when along came a human equivalent. She was a little lady who appeared old but was probably not as old as she looked. She was certainly very hesitant and diffident. It was difficult to judge who was going to be more submissive, Hopeless or our lady visitor. However, she seemed very kind and very gentle and very worried about doing the right things, so Helen felt that she was the best person for Hopeless to go to.

Loving care

I will never forget the loving care in which Helen brought me and my brothers and sisters up, so that we were able to start life with the ability to socialise with other dogs and with humans, in a way that gave us such a good start. Since Helen worked with my new owners, I often met her, and my mother, but eventually she and her daughters left the area, though I will never ever forget them.

Mother's disquiet

We dogs live in the here and now. Obviously, we are influenced by the past; it builds up a sub-conscious memory bank which affects the way in which we react, but we do not dwell on it. Equally, we have no concept of the future. We are just happy to take each day as it comes. Nonetheless, we have a deeply ingrained sixth sense which enables us to react to a problem instinctively, without really knowing why we are doing so.

Looking back, my mother had this sixth sense; particularly when it came to the potential owners of her puppies. She had obviously shown her disquiet with several of the people buying us. Events were to prove she had been right in her concerns.

Before I tell you about my own wonderful life, let me tell you what happened to my brothers and sister.

Chapter Two

Patch's nightmare

A bad start

My brother, Patch, was bought by a family with a young, petulant, spoilt son. We had hated being fondled by him since he would surreptitiously pinch us. His father was obviously spoiling his son by buying him the puppy he wanted for Christmas, but the father really had no empathy or understanding. The boy had an older sister who my brothers and sisters all liked. She was kind, considerate, and had a natural empathy for understanding how we puppies were feeling as we were wrenched away from our mother and Helen, and, instead, taken off by total strangers.

As Patch disappeared with his new owners, he looked justifiably worried. Had he been bought for the sister, life might have been fine. The sister did her best to reassure and comfort Patch, but her brother was in charge and clearly was setting out to enjoy making Patch's life a misery.

No consideration

Thus, when they got home, there was no thought of taking Patch into the garden to 'be clean' as had happened to me. Everyone charged into the house. The daughter did ask if she could take Patch for a run in the garden, but she was shot down by a very irritable father who told her—in no uncertain terms—that it was her brother's dog and she should not interfere.

The excitement of leaving home, being taken on a car drive and then deposited in a strange house with two grown-ups who had no concept of how to treat a puppy, meant that Patch found himself bursting to go to the toilet. Conscious of our mum's training, he did his best to find somewhere suitable. He found what he thought was a suitable area in a corner behind the sitting room door. This was quickly spotted by the father who became angry, shouted loudly, grabbed Patch, took him to the mess he had made, and pushed his nose into it, while hitting him hard. Then he was carried out and thrown into the garden where he was left by himself, for what seemed to be an eternity.

By the time Patch was allowed in, the family were beginning to get ready to go and see some of their relatives prior to Christmas. The daughter very sensibly suggested that she ought to be allowed to take Patch out for a little run before going on another car journey. She was shot down by an irritable father who said that Patch had already spent long enough in the garden so he didn't need to have a walk. The daughter suggested that it would be far kinder to leave

Patch behind and settle him down in an outhouse, with some rugs, and with some newspapers as a toilet area. Again, she was told not to interfere and her brother proudly carried Patch into the family's Jag, surreptitiously pulling and pushing him about, and pinching him when he could.

By then, they had started on their journey and the motion of the car, the irritation by the boy, and the fact that Patch had spent so long in the garden, meant that he could not contain himself, and had an 'accident'. To the father, this was the final straw. He screeched into a lay-by, opened his car window, leant over the back of his car seat, grabbed Patch, turned, and threw him out of the car, across the other side of the road into the path of a large lorry.

Saved by lorry driver

The lorry driver could do nothing but bring his lorry to a stop as soon as he could. He ran back but could not find the pup. Eventually he heard whimpering from some rough ground on the side of the road. Somehow, his wheels had avoided Patch, who, once the lorry had stopped, had been able to crawl off the road.

The way in which the father had so wickedly thrown Patch meant that his paws and tummy was badly grazed with some of his paws bleeding. The lorry driver gently wrapped Patch into his pullover and drove to a nearby pub where he knew the landlady.

She was exceptionally kind. She took charge of Patch, rang for a vet, reported the incident to the local policeman, and set about caring properly for the young puppy. The vet arrived, dealt with the injuries he had suffered, gave him a mild injection to calm him down, and another antibiotic injection to prevent the injuries turning septic.

The father had barely stopped while throwing Patch out of the car and had immediately screeched away at top speed. The son was so twisted that he thought it was all great fun. The mother and her daughter were in tears, which angered the father even more. He gave up the idea of going to see the family for Christmas, turned the car around and went home by an alternative route to avoid being recognised.

Gwen's loving care

Apparently, the lady at the pub was called Gwen. Over the years, she had had a succession of dogs all of whom had had loving homes. Her last dog had died of old age some four or five months earlier, so Gwen was only too happy to care for Patch. He was given a nice warm bed in an outhouse with an 'accidents' corner. The vet came until his wounds were healed and Patch began to enjoy the life of a much-loved pet.

Gwen's husband had died so she had to run the pub, but she always gave Patch a walk first thing in the morning, in the mid-afternoon, and last thing at night.

However, he didn't lack exercise. Quite a few older customers of the pub had also had dogs that had died of old age. These customers felt they were too old to take on another dog themselves, so they happily vied with each other to give Patch regular walks. One customer even bought a tennis racket and a supply of balls, so that in a nearby field he could hit the ball hard enough for Patch to chase after it at great speed.

When the weather was fine, Patch would be tethered on a long lead in an outside courtyard with tables and chairs, so he had the interest of watching customers coming and going, many of whom would tickle his ears, or rub his tummy, or encourage Patch to lie down and keep them company.

So, after a disastrous start, he began to have a good life with lots of tender loving care.

Gwen's illness

Initially, Patch was really happy. He had a loving owner who was very much the leader, so Patch felt comfortable that he 'knew his place'. In fact, with frequent walks, and in particular a walk late at night and early in the morning, Patch was soon clean.

Life could not have been more perfect, but then Patch began to sense that Gwen was not very well. He picked up that she had a very faint smell about her. One thing I did understand was that we dogs, by smelling the odours of our humans, we can recognise their emotional state and even recognise when our human is unwell.

Certainly, by picking up the odours which Gwen was emitting, Patch became very worried. He picked up that she was also worried; that she was not herself. Then she took Patch with her when she went down to the doctor and emerged even more worried. Patch had already realised that she was ill and unhappy, now she had broken down and was crying. Patch felt dreadful, he tried to help by nuzzling against her, and licking her. She appreciated his gestures. But, when other humans came in, they didn't understand and he was pushed into the scullery out of the way, which made Patch extremely unhappy and he whimpered softly to himself because he could not comfort her.

Another life

Patch went through a dreadful few weeks. When Gwen was by herself, he could cuddle against her and even sleep on her bed to give her comfort. When other people appeared, he was banished.

He was rescued when one of the regulars of the pub, who had often caressed Patch, came to see Gwen and offered Patch 'a good home'. Given her illness, it was a worry off her mind to feel that he would be settled into a new home.

Police dog

In fact, the man who had offered him a good home was a policeman, working as a police dog handler.

Initially, it was all a bit strange, and, having been used to sleeping on Gwen's bed, Patch was rather shattered to find himself living in a kennel environment. However, he eventually settled down, began to appreciate the friendship of the dogs in the adjoining kennels, and enjoy his training.

Sniffer dog

Because we collies have a really acute sense of smell, Patch was trained to be a sniffer dog. Because he was with his first owners so briefly, they had not given him a name, and as Gwen had tended to call him 'Sweetheart', he was renamed as Fred.

Starting work

He was happier once he had completed his training and became a fully qualified sniffer dog. He travelled in an air-conditioned van with a thick carpet on the floor and found the work of going into buildings to see whether there were any problems, great fun. I gathered that he had had to search for danger and was praised by his owner for the intensity with which he carried out his searches, and for his obedience.

Visit delayed

When Fred was first trained and was still quite young, he did blot his copybook. Prior to a visit of a noted dignitary, he indicated that there was something suspicious about an ornamental well. So, emergency procedures were put in place and the visit delayed.

To his handler's embarrassment, the 'dangerous object' was somebody's half-eaten pork pie. However, when Fred retired after nine years of service, his sergeant said it had been a pleasure working with such a steady, faithful dog who had given a lot of people peace of mind over the years.

Retirement

Once Fred retired, he went to live with his sergeant as the family pet, which he enjoyed; though he missed going out 'to work'.

Chapter Three

Hopeless's short life

Hopeless 'takes over'

The lady who had bought our sister, Hopeless, was rather small, quietly-spoken and extremely diffident. She had decided to get a dog because her sister, who had been very dominant, had just died. Hopeless had been renamed as Sally and she quickly sensed that her new owner was so upset by the death of her sister, that she was in no fit state to be assertive. Sally (Hopeless) took over.

Her new owner was desperate for love; fed Sally titbits, took her for walks around the garden, in fact whenever Sally stood impatiently at the back door, she was taken for a walk. Sally became the centre of her owner's attention, all day, every day and was not prepared to be ignored. She was playing the role of leader, demanding obedience.

Jealousy

Sally took great exception to the frequency with which her owner answered the telephone, and the length of time she spent talking to her various friends. She began to attack the legs of the table on which the telephone stood. So, her owner stood the table legs in tin cans so that she could not damage them. Frustrated, Sally tried to bite and scratch the carpet. When this was ignored, she tried a loud high-pitched growl. This effectively ended the conversation and Sally sought to deter future phone calls by guarding the telephone.

Unwelcome visitor

Sally's first experience of other dogs outside her own litter came when she was 14 weeks old. A family friend brought his 12-month-old dog puppy to 'play' with her. The dog puppy was very large and boisterous and pestered Sally unmercifully, despite all her efforts at submission. Her owner, mistaking Sally's actions as play let the puppies get on with their 'game'. At last, in desperation, Sally flung herself at her tormentor, snapping and growling. The larger puppy backed off in surprise as Sally's owner rushed to comfort her, using words of praise. In a few seconds, Sally had learned that a display of aggression not only discouraged a potential aggressor, but also gained the instant attention and praise of her owner.

This episode, however, made her owner realise that she had perhaps been wrong not to help Sally socialise with other dogs. So, she contacted a local dog club trainer who suggested that she take Sally to one of his training sessions. On the first evening, Sally jumped quite happily out of the car and followed her mistress to the hall where the class was in progress. She found herself in an echoing room full of barking dogs. It was all too much for her. She slipped her lead, ran back to the car, and cowered underneath it. Eventually with the help of the trainer, her mistress was able to drag her out and back into the hall, where she spent the entire evening shivering under a chair.

If it had been recognised at this point that Sally needed to be introduced gradually to non-threatening dogs in a calm and friendly environment, it is likely that her story would have had a different ending.

Out of date trainer

The next week, Sally was again dragged, very reluctantly, into the hall where she immediately hid under the chair of her mistress. Had the trainer had the sense to choose another, somewhat submissive, dog and let them meet each other quietly in the corner of the hall, it might have worked. Instead he did the opposite, Sally was pulled into the middle of the room so that other dogs could get to know her. It was the worst possible thing for the trainer to do. He should have had more sense.

As the first, somewhat dominant, dog approached, Sally tried desperately to escape but couldn't, as she was restrained by her lead. She had already learned from her large and very boisterous visitor, that submission was ineffective. So she tried aggression. She flung herself at the advancing threat, growling ferociously. The dog's startled owner quickly pulled him back while her owner petted Sally to calm her. Again, Sally's aggression had been rewarded.

Her owner tried to have one final attempt but as soon as she was dragged, again reluctantly, into the hall, her demeanour changed. She lunged forward, to the end of the lead, intent on repelling any possible threat before it could approach her. Her mistress could not restrain her.

Punishment

The trainer ran up and grabbed her lead. Sally tried to bite him. Unfortunately, the trainer had no knowledge of the different causes of aggression, or of the appropriate methods of treatment, so he decided to 'teach her a lesson' using the age-old method, a good hiding. Sally learned the lesson. She learned that strangers could be just as threatening and unpredictable as dogs – and she already knew how to deal with them!

During the following weeks, Sally began to show signs of fear whenever she was approached by anyone she did not know.

Ignorant brother

Her mistress had a brother who thought he was something of an expert on how to handle dogs, so he said he would take her out. His approach was, again, using the age-old method of subjugation, to which Sally reacted badly. A well-meaning neighbour tried to intervene to calm her down but got badly bitten for his pains.

The 'know-it-all' brother told his sister, 'Sally should be taken to the vet and put down'. Had her mistress been able to talk quietly to the vet's behaviour therapist, it is likely that she could have been persuaded to adopt his or her recommendations and give Sally the time and patience to overcome her fears. But, Sally's mistress had always been submissive and was bullied by her brother into putting her to sleep.

An unavoidable tragedy

Sally was just seven months old when she was killed. It was a totally avoidable tragedy. The shy lady should never have considered buying a collie. We are very demanding, intense dogs and it was obvious to us that the lady buying Hopeless would not be able to cope. The ideal dog for someone like her would have been a much smaller dog.

Chapter Four

Pinky's wasted life

Just a dog?

Some humans feel that a dog is 'just a dog'; just an animal to be treated like any other animal. The idea that a dog can give and receive affection and want to be able, need to be able, to do something worthwhile for their owner, would almost certainly result in scornful laughter from the human concerned.

A dog is *not* a baby

Many humans who have something lacking in their own lives, want to treat a dog as their 'baby'. They want to mollycoddle and spoil their 'baby'. As a result, these 'spoilt babies' turn into problem dogs who try to dominate their owners by trying to act as 'the pack leader'. Too often, this becomes such a problem, that the dog has to be taken to the vet. The owners, who feel guilty, try to minimise what they have done by talking about putting their dog to sleep. But, it is a sleep that it is truly a death sentence.

Over-protective owners

Some well-meaning owners are over protective of their dog. They might have had experience of the old-fashioned 'trainer' who had the philosophy that dogs were subservient animals which had to do what they were told, when they were told, immediately they were told, or face the prospect of physical punishment.

Indeed, the reason that my poor sister, Hopeless, ended up having an early death was because, in good faith, her mistress had submitted her to just such an experience. It is understandable that anyone who has had experience of this type of 'training', which is really abuse, would not wish to subject their own dog to such a procedure.

Unkind owners

Some owners themselves become unkind, if not cruel, by their failure to find a kind way of teaching their dog how to behave. We see it, my dad, mum and I, almost every day in our lane.

We, and our neighbours, have cars which go up and down our lane; we have visitors, and tradesmen come to deliver. So, whenever my dad, or mum, take me for a walk down the lane, we are likely to meet a car.

My hearing was more acute than Dad's when I was younger, and quite often I would go to him and give him a nudge in case he had not heard a car coming. He would then point to the side of the road and give the command, 'off'. I would move onto the verge and sit still until the car had passed. If I was some way in front of or behind Dad, as soon as he saw a car, he would give a sharp whistle, point me to the side of the road and while he probably said 'off', all I needed was to see his outstretched arm. I would move off the road, and sit on the verge.

This was the behaviour of a dog who knew how to behave. But I see many owners who have not taught their dogs how to behave; they pull them across the lane, almost suffocating them in the process, to get them to go up on the verge; quite often helping the process by kicking them up their bottoms! As a dog, I do not feel it is the right way for them to be treated and I cannot understand owners for whom this type of treatment is preferable to the way I have been trained, to respond of my own free will.

Mistreatment

More importantly, an untrained dog is more likely to get into trouble.

We were driving down our lane in our car recently, when we slowed right down to pass a man with his dog. The man went onto the verge and squatted down with his dog—which was good—but he then shot his arm forward which I would have taken to be a command to go. His dog certainly took it to be a command to go, whereupon his owner pulled him back and started smacking him for being 'disobedient'. In my view, it was the man who needed a smack, firstly for not training his dog to sit as I have been trained, and secondly for punishing the dog for his own mistake.

I do wish that humans would accept that a dog which has not been taught how to behave is fundamentally an unhappy dog that doesn't understand what it is being asked to do, and why it is punished as a result.

My brother Pinky

My brother, Pinky, had been lucky in the sense that he had gone to a good home with well-meaning people. Because we collies are particularly sensitive and can react to the 'body language' of our owners, Pinky had managed to understand what was expected of him, but had never been properly trained. As a result of this lack of training, and his owners' lack of consistency, Pinky, lost his life. Let me tell you the story.

Dad and Mum often called in to see Helen on their way home from the office, to collect or deliver the work which she did on her computer for them. So, I was able to see Jess, my mother, on a regular basis. She, in turn, did her best via the 'doggy grapevine' to keep in touch with my brothers and sisters.

One day, when we got to Helen's, my natural mother, Jess, was nowhere to be seen. Eventually I found her hiding in the corner of a barn, in a dreadfully upset state. She could barely speak to me. After a time she told me that while in town with Helen, they had heard a dog screaming in agony. So, they went to see what was wrong.

It was Pinky lying in a crumpled heap with his two distraught owners and a small crowd of equally-upset dog lovers—some in tears—frustrated by their inability to help. When he saw Jess, Pinky did his best to speak but his words still came out as a whimpering scream. Plaintively, he kept repeating, 'He told me to go on—for Pete's sake, go on'.

For Pete's sake, come on!

The owner told Helen that although he had Pinky on a lead, he was dragging behind, so he had turned round and said sharply, 'For Pete's sake, come *on*'. Apparently, when he was walking Pinky around the village and crossing lanes, he would first call Pinky 'to heel' and when the coast was clear, tell him to 'go on'. So Pinky had got in the habit of shooting away to enjoy himself whenever told to 'go on'.

Hence, when his owner, in town, had said, 'For Pete's sake, come *on*', he hadn't heard the preceding words, he'd merely picked up that one word, 'on', and charged forward; straight into the side of a passing car.

Terrible injuries

Mum couldn't bear to describe his injuries to me. After an eternity, a vet came, gave one look, quickly prepared and gave an injection which silenced Pinky—for good. I lay down with Jess, trying to provide some comfort by my closeness, but—all too soon—Dad whistled for me and I had to go.

Lack of understanding

On the way home, I reflected on how sad it was that Pinky's two owners had not understood that we dogs do not speak English; we hear sounds. When his owners made the sound 'go on', it was normally to give him permission to go on ahead. The fact that on this sad occasion they had told him to 'come on' was lost on him. Forgetting he was on a lead, he took in that he was being encouraged to shoot on ahead as when walking free around the village.

We dogs wish we could get it across to humans that *we don't understand words.* We associate certain sounds with certain actions. In Pinky's case he associated 'on' with shooting forward—with tragic results.

If his owners had shouted 'heel' he would have known what to do. More importantly, if his owners had been consistent in keeping him to heel until they had safely crossed any form of road or lane, it would not have entered his head to charge forward.

We dogs do wish humans would be more consistent in thinking through some of their bad habits, when they inadvertently encourage us and for which we suffer. Pinky paid with his life. Sad.

True kindness

True kindness is based on humans who have the willingness, and the ability, to teach their dogs how to behave so that the owners, and their dogs, can have a much more enjoyable, fulfilling life.

Let me make it clear, we dogs feel that owners who do not teach us how to behave are letting us down, are unkind in expecting us to react when we haven't been taught properly to do so, and the result of their actions can often cause the early death of their bemused dogs.

Let me give you a far better example.

Shopping in Exeter

We, my dad, mum and me, had gone shopping in Exeter. Put more accurately, my mum had gone shopping in Exeter with my dad as her chauffeur and with me helping to keep Dad company! While she was shopping, my dad took me for a walk, which ended up with him sitting on a bench along the river. There was plenty of activity both in the river and along the adjoining footpaths, so both he and I were very interested and happy.

Meeting Daisy and Vonnie

I was intrigued when a miniature Yorkshire terrier came trotting along who seemed full of vim and vigour and the joys of life! I was particularly fascinated by the very smart red coat she was wearing. Her owner obviously decided that she too would sit down on the bench, so, while she talked to my dad, I was able to talk to the interesting young bitch, called Daisy. She did not really want to talk about it, but apparently she had had a very unhappy young life with several different owners and had ended up in a rescue centre, totally bemused and confused about what was happening to her.

Then one day, two very nice ladies came along. One was a vet who gave her a thorough check-over, the other was a dog trainer, who (like the lady who had bought my sister Clever Clogs) had set about getting to know her better. She had got Daisy to stand so that she could be stroked gently and played a few simple games with her to see how she reacted. Daisy had really enjoyed her time with the two ladies, so she was delighted when they put her on a lead, led her to their car and lifted her onto the back seat to take her to her new home.

Daisy was a bit worried about what was going to happen but the two ladies had built a rapport with her and she felt she could trust them, whatever happened. However, she was a bit puzzled when—after a pleasant drive—she was walked into a house and introduced to a lovely lady called Betty, who also immediately built a rapport with Daisy by lifting her onto her lap and giving her a cuddle and then taking her into the garden for an exciting game. In fact, by the end of the game Daisy had really fallen for Betty and happily followed her into the house grinning as if she had, at long last, found a real family.

Learning to behave

Daisy thoroughly enjoyed being with Betty, who took her for regular walks, played with her in the garden, gave her a nice warm bed, and—most importantly—gave her lots of cuddles. When she went out for a walk, she was learning about the everyday sounds of traffic and was encouraged to meet and talk to other dogs in the park and generally taught to appreciate reacting with other dogs and people. She was also taught to accept the everyday noises of the home and the environment in which her new owner, Betty, lived.

(Daisy didn't realise it but my dad told me that she was going through a training procedure known as 'socialising', where volunteers, like Betty, offer time, love and commitment, by turning boisterous youngsters into well-rounded, well-behaved, sociable dogs.)

The ladies belonged to an organisation called 'Hearing Dogs for Deaf People'.

Kennels!

Daisy told me that she had become really happy and contented with Betty and was beginning to fall in love with her. She was therefore totally shattered when, one day, one of the original ladies she had met came, took her in the car, and stopped outside a range of buildings, where she was met by a really lovely girl called Sarah. Sarah took her for a walk, played a game or two with her, sat down on the ground and gave her a nice cuddle and generally tried to reassure her. Nonetheless, Daisy was still rather taken aback when she took her into a run fenced off with wire netting and with a wooden box at the end of the run, which, when Daisy investigated, she found to have a really warm, comfortable bed.

Having been used to the family life with Betty, she found it something of a shock to be in a kennel environment. It helped that she could watch Sarah going to and fro and she had the companionship of the dogs in the runs on either side of her, but it was still a shock.

Training

Next morning, Daisy was delighted when Sarah came to let her out of the kennel and took her for a walk again. But she then took Daisy into what seemed to be a house with the normal facilities of a lounge, a bedroom, a kitchen, and a hallway.

Everyday, Sarah would come to take Daisy out for a run and a game and then take her back into the 'house' where she was taught how she should react to certain sounds such as a doorbell. She was taught that when she heard the noise of the doorbell she should run to Sarah and scratch her legs vigorously; when Sarah put both her hands out in a gesture which was saying, 'What is it?', Daisy was taught that she had to lead Sarah to the source of the noise.

While it took Daisy some time to adjust to living in a kennel, she thoroughly enjoyed her daily training sessions with Sarah, particularly the time she spent in the house, where Sarah taught her how to react to a number of different sounds. Each time, Daisy had to run to Sarah and ensure her attention by scratching vigorously at her legs before leading Sarah to the source of the sounds, such as the telephone. As soon as she so, did she was given her reward of a titbit. At one point, Sarah got into bed so that, when the alarm went, Daisy could jump on the bed and, in effect, wake her up. Again she was given her titbit when she did so.

There was a stage in her daily training where she was taught that if the fire alarm went off, she had first to attract Sarah's attention, and then lie down, without moving, on the floor and refuse to move on the basis that it was a fire alarm, and it would be dangerous for Daisy to lead her into the fire. Again she got a titbit.

A game

Daisy found all these different exercises almost like a game, which she thoroughly enjoyed, particularly when she was rewarded whenever she did the right thing. Daisy thought the trainers were very clever; they worked out what would most please the dog they were training, and then gave the dog concerned that particular reward.

This could be a piece of food, the chance to play with a toy, a cuddle, or, in some cases, a brushing. Sarah worked out that Daisy most liked having a cuddle, so whenever she deserved a reward, that's what she got.

Daisy did not realise it, but she was being taught the sounds needed by the lady who was to become her eventual owner.

An attractive lady

At one of the initial training sessions Daisy had, there had been a very attractive lady sitting in, who was obviously very keen to be friendly with her. In fact, she took her for one or two walks by herself to get to know her better. At the time, Daisy thought nothing of it and, frankly, was more concerned about playing with Sarah. However, the lady was going to be her eventual owner.

After a training period of some weeks, Daisy was a bit surprised when, instead of her normal daily training sessions with Sarah, the attractive lady she had met before took over her training, supervised by Sarah. She was very friendly, keen to make friends with Daisy, and started taking her out. Her name was Von and when she started taking Daisy out for more walks than Sarah, Daisy started to look out for her visits.

After a few days, instead of taking Daisy for a walk, Von put her into her car and took her to her new home. Daisy was really pleased to get back to living in a proper home and settled in quite quickly with her new owner.

A happy loving home

She was now a really happy dog. She had a nice home and she thought Von was a really lovely lady, and rapidly fell in love with her. It was a two-way thing. Von was delighted to have the company, the friendship and the help that Daisy could give her, while Daisy was delighted to feel useful and to be able to help her lovely new owner. Initially, Daisy was just dealing with the sounds to which Sarah had taught her to react. But, as she progressively got to understand what Von needed, Daisy started to pick up some other sounds which would be useful for Von to hear, and so extended her ability to help her beloved mistress.

Impressed

As soon as we met my mum, I heard my dad telling her with great enthusiasm about how we had met a miniature Yorkshire terrier called Daisy and her mum, Vonnie. I heard my dad saying that he was particularly impressed with two points. First, Hearing Dogs for Deaf People made a point of trying to use as many 'rescue dogs' as possible and secondly, that all the training was reward based.

Burning bacon

Apparently, Vonnie had told him a funny story. Not long after Daisy had joined her, she was cooking bacon in the kitchen. Daisy realised that the smoke alarm was sounding, raced in to her, and jumped at her. On being asked 'What is it?' Daisy had dropped to the floor, which is what she was trained to do in the event of danger. As Vonnie was trying to discover what was wrong, a neighbour came in to tell her that the smoke alarm had been triggered by burning bacon. Vonnie thanked her neighbour, turned off the alarm, and carried on cooking. What she had not realised was that the alarm was connected to the central office at the fire station.

Burly firefighters

A few moments later Daisy came back into the kitchen to alert Vonnie again, this time leading her to the window. The sight that greeted Vonnie was amazing—two fire engines and twelve burly firefighters were standing in her driveway. The firemen insisted on having a photograph with Daisy, and were very impressed with her skills.

Vonnie told the fireman that she was very, very pleased that she was fortunate enough to have such a helpful, loving, funny, faithful little friend. She told the firemen that she felt herself very lucky to be the recipient of a hearing dog and particularly lucky that it was Daisy.

The solitude of deafness

Vonnie told the firemen that before she had Daisy she was shopping in a supermarket and suddenly realised that she was the only person in the shop. Apparently, the fire alarm had been sounded and every employee and customer had hurriedly left the shop, leaving her isolated. Similarly, she had once been trying on some clothes in the changing room of a dress shop when, again, she suddenly found herself alone. Again, a fire alarm had gone off and, in the rush to evacuate the building, the shop assistant had not remembered that she was in the changing room.

Vonnie tried to explain to the firemen that when you are deaf, you feel terribly alone and isolated. For her, Daisy was a constant, loving, kind, amusing companion with whom she could play games. Her walks had more purpose now that she had Daisy and Daisy's arrival had changed her life forever.

My brother Pinky lost his life because his owners felt it was 'wrong' to train him. My namesake, Daisy, could so easily have been 'put to sleep' by her original owners. But instead she became a highly-trained, loving and much loved helper.

Chapter Five

Nosey's novice owners

My brother, Nosey, had been purchased by an elderly couple. When Helen was talking to the gentleman, he had said that now that he was retired, he wanted to walk regularly but felt that if he was by himself, the women he passed might be worried by seeing a solitary male, but would find it far more acceptable if the man was walking with a dog. In short, he was not buying a dog because he wanted a dog, but merely wanted to justify his walk.

Disinterest

He did not really give Nosey any attention or stimulation. He was kept on a lead—admittedly an extending lead—but still a lead, which meant that he could not run around enjoying himself. Whenever the man saw another dog coming, Nosey would be pulled up tight against the man's legs unable to pass the time of day with the other dog. If Nosey wanted to do the normal doggy things such as lifting his leg, or doing what my dad called a 'big job' the man was embarrassed and intolerant of the time taken and obviously hated the idea of having to use a doggy bag.

Company

When I first joined my new owners, I was keen to keep them company wherever they moved; either going to see what Dad was doing, or going to see what Mum was doing. The wife of Nosey's new owner found this intolerable. As he tried to keep them company, she screamed at him, asking her husband, 'Why can't this dog lie down out of the way?' Eventually they bought a playpen. This wasn't too bad in the sense that he could watch what they were doing but it restricted his ability to move around.

Exercise

My dad was keen to give me any opportunity for a bit of exercise. If he had to go out to the garage, or down the garden, I would go with him. Certainly, if he went down to the village, I would scoot up the steps, scoot off into the woods and then scoot back in time to get in the car and go with him. Obviously, if the ground was wet, Dad would wipe my feet thoroughly before I went back into the house.

Nosey's mistress was fanatical about the cleanliness of her house, and refused to let her husband take Nosey out with him for these odd jaunts like me, because, 'It would get her floors dirty'. So, Nosey was limited to three set walks a day. But, if he was asleep out of boredom when the man decided to go for a walk, his wife would often say, 'If that dog's asleep, clearly he doesn't need a walk'. The fact that poor Nosey would have been desperate for a walk and was merely sleeping out of boredom, didn't count.

Tyranny of noise

If humans are made ill by the stress of the noises they hear, then, since our hearing is twice that of humans, we dogs have twice the problem. If some humans become ill and even die from noise, what would the impact be on us dogs?

The owners of my brother, Nosey, had absolutely no understanding or sympathy on this issue. They had an elderly mother who was deaf and wanted the television on loud. This was torture for Nosey. Because his owners did not appreciate the sensitivity of his hearing, he was bellowed at to try to get him to behave. In fact, like any other dog, he was so confused by the shouts that he did not know what to do. He would move around the sitting room trying to escape the noise. His owners would get cross, yell at him to lie down, and would sometimes smack him for not lying down. Ultimately, they started leaving him out in the kitchen.

Problems ignored

Whenever Nosey had a problem, he would try to get his owners' attention but either the man, the woman, or both, would shout at him and exclaim to each other, 'What's wrong with that dog?' and tell him with some annoyance to sit down and not be a nuisance. If he persisted, he would be shut out in the kitchen. If he then became sick or had an accident of some sort, they might realise that he had been trying to get help. But, instead of feeling sorry for him, and trying to make good their lack of understanding, they would be cross with him for having had the accident, which he had been trying to avoid! Moreover, the next time Nosey might have a problem, they would both be equally obtuse; still make no effort to understand what he was trying to explain; and again—tell him off—for asking for their help.

Cruel owners?

I am sure that Nosey's owners did not regard themselves as 'cruel'. He was fed regularly. He had a warm, comfortable bed. He was taken for three walks a day. Occasionally, he might be taken out when they went for a drive in their car. In one sense he was a 'member of the family' but in another he never felt that he 'belonged'. He was treated more like an animated ornament.

Life changed

Then, one day, his life was changed dramatically. Their daughter came to stay. Nosey did not understand who she was, or where she had come from, it was sufficient for him that she was there; particularly when she immediately fell in love with him. For the first time in his life, he started getting lots of lovely cuddles and kisses. She bought him some toys with which he could play in the house. Her grandmother was not too pleased but she obviously loved her granddaughter and so progressively became more relaxed about these things.

Her father was going through a spell of bad health, so the daughter started taking Nosey for his regular walks. When the father had taken him for walks, he had to amuse himself since his owner would walk along giving Nosey little or no attention. The daughter involved Nosey fully, she would give him a race by running; and then she bought a tennis ball and threw it for him. For the first time in his life, he was going for a walk with somebody who really wanted to share the walk with him.

He quickly fell in love with her. For the first time, life became fun. He felt loved and wanted. So, when she disappeared again, he was heartbroken when life went back to normal. The contrast between life with his owners and life with the daughter, was almost too much to bear.

So when, a few weeks later, the doorbell went and the daughter returned, Nosey was ecstatic with joy. Nosey was a bit slow, but he eventually worked out that she was living and working not far away and was keen to visit her parents and elderly grandparents as often as possible, and because she enjoyed her times with Nosey.

Change of attitude

It became apparent that Nosey's owners had not previously owned a dog, and didn't really know how to behave. When they saw how happy Nosey became when he was with their daughter and, very importantly, how much fun she had with Nosey, they began to relax. The man started playing with Nosey when he took him for walks, and even started to play with him in the garden. The woman started giving him a friendly pat and—over time—a friendly cuddle.

The daughter had told them about the fact that Nosey had a particularly acute sense of hearing so much so that he found the noise of the television a torture. Up to that point, the woman's very elderly mother had refused to wear a hearing aid. Once she realised the problem, she started to wear one. In fact, she bought a set of earphones which enabled her to listen to the television without bothering the family, or Nosey. In fact, Nosey became very affectionate with her and often kept her company, which made the grandmother particularly keen that she did nothing which would upset her beloved pet, Nosey.

Member of the family

So, the arrival of the granddaughter, and her regular visits, totally changed the atmosphere. Nosey became a much-loved member of the family. However, the grandmother smoked heavily which did not help Nosey. She also spoilt him by feeding him chocolate, which can poison us dogs.

When the parents took Nosey to the vet they were aware

that their parent smoked, but they did not know and were shocked to learn that pets exposed to tobacco smoke could develop cancer. They also didn't know that their mother was giving Nosey so much chocolate in secret. It was making him ill. He was so ill that the vet was worried about his survival. But survive he did and, eventually, was allowed home.

The grandmother felt so guilty about the harm she had done to Nosey that she became his devoted carer, stopped giving him chocolate; and gave up smoking! So, Nosey once again became a very happy and much-loved dog; especially when the daughter was home.

Chapter Six

The Bully's terrible life

Taken in

Looking back, I think that Helen was rather taken in by the man who came to buy The Bully. The man was smartly dressed, with charming manners, and said all the right things, in the right way. But our mother was very unhappy and tried to shepherd The Bully away from the man. In fact, Mum must have had a sixth sense because she muttered to me that the man was 'evil'. To be fair to her, Helen was always very careful about those to whom she let her beloved dogs go, but she must have been really taken in by his charm because he was allowed to buy the dog we had called The Bully.

This was a puppy-type name, and in the light of what happened to my brother, I now feel very guilty that we were so unkind. So, let me call my brother by the name Pete, which he was given by his new owner.

A good owner

Initially, he was very considerate. He renamed The Bully as Pete and bought some turf to grass over a corner of the garden, which the newly-named Pete could use to go to the toilet. He recognised that until a dog is at least six months old, they cannot control themselves overnight, and so provided a bed in an adjoining outhouse with a corner for a plentiful supply of papers as a toilet. He fed him quite well and took him for quite a few walks each day and would take him in the garden to throw a ball for him.

A terrible owner

Then, his owner would change totally and appear to lose all interest in Pete, who would spend most of the day tied up in the outhouse with a few short interludes to go to the toilet. Walks and games became a thing of the past. When Pete was allowed in the house, instead of being petted, the man seemed to take every opportunity to be unkind. Pete didn't know what to make of this, if he found himself ahead of his owner, he would get a deliberate kick on the lower part of his legs. In fact, Pete developed a limp because one of the kicks he received must have cracked a bone. Pete could never work out what the man wanted to do next, but if he had the misfortune of ending up in front of his owner, he was kneed out of the way, often so violently that he could be knocked sideways.

Loving not enough

The only gift we dogs have is the gift of love. All Pete could do was to try and give love, to be friendly and affectionate, whenever the man was in a good mood. When he wasn't, all our brother could do was to try to keep out of the way.

Mood swings

The man must have been ill because his mood swings became more and more violent. There would be periods when he could be very affectionate and almost loving and he and Pete would have a whale of a time with plenty of walks and games. Then there would be other periods when the man would be in a deep depression and if Pete did not get out of the way, and stay out of the way, his life would be a misery. He could spend long periods in the outhouse tied on a relatively short lead so that he could barely move and there were periods when he was either not fed at all, or fed very spasmodically.

The climax

Finally, a day came when the man was obviously in a really foul mood, shouting and swearing and bashing dishes and furniture around. Normally when the man got into a really bad mood, Pete would disappear into a hideaway under the stairs and hope that the man would forget that he existed. This particular morning the man had closed the doors in the kitchen so that Pete could not escape.

Initially he hid under the table, but when he thought that the man was about to open the door into the garden, he tried to shoot out. The man had a large saucepan full of hot fat which, he claimed, he was taking out to the compost. He was already in a rage, which he took out on poor Pete by deliberately tipping the boiling hot fat over him. In the fracas, the door to the garden had become opened and Pete ran madly around in circles trying to escape the terrible pain. His owner did nothing but swear at him for getting in the way.

Good Samaritans

Nobody knew what to do. An elderly neighbour was able to steer Pete into his grandchildren's sandpit where the sand was very wet and very cold; his wife came out with several towels she had damped with water and eventually they were able to get Pete into their car and take him to the vet.

He had lost all the hair down his backbone and spent some time being treated at the vets. This could have cost a great deal of money but the elderly couple offered to help and the local newspaper appealed for funds for his treatment, while the vets did a lot of the work at a concessionary rate.

Eventually Pete made a complete recovery.

By now, the elderly couple had really fallen in love with him, and he with them, so they all settled down with what they hoped would be a long and happy life together.

Pete's former owner had been renting his house and, in view of his actions had disappeared.

Fatal illness

The lady caring for Pete had not enjoyed good health for some time. In fact, it was the husband who spent time looking after the wife. Then he became ill. The woman was, understandably, totally shattered and spent most of her time by her husband's bed. A friendly neighbour did his best to look after Pete but he, too, was infirm and could only feed him and give him a few short walks during the course of the day.

The nephew

While the elderly couple had done their best, they could just not cope. But, trying to do their best for Pete, they gave a generous amount of money to one of their nephews on the basis that he would take over and care for him.

Initially, all went well. The nephew, called Julian, was unemployed and only too happy to give Pete plenty of walks. Pete was a bit concerned that he was left at home every night while Julian went out with his friends; often returning quite late. In addition, Julian's lifestyle of going out late in the evening, and staying in bed in the morning, meant that Pete was fed on a rather inconsistent basis. Nonetheless, Julian was friendly enough without really displaying any empathy for Pete.

A job

Then, Julian got a job. He had to leave every morning by half past seven. Since he stopped for a drink on the way home, he was rarely home before half past six. It was a very long day. Julian gave Pete a short walk before he left. His mother came in and gave Pete a longer walk around ten o'clock and a friend had a key to give him a walk around two o'clock, but then it seemed a very long wait until Julian got home in the early evening.

Boredom

Pete found the afternoon dragged on. He was bored and frustrated. For something to do, he started chewing a chair leg. It wasn't much fun, but at least it was something to do. When he heard Julian coming up the stairs in the evening, he was really delighted and went to the door, nuzzling at the door handle, and wagging his tail, ready to greet Julian. Initially, Julian responded and started to tickle his ears. Then he froze. He had seen the damage to his chair legs.

Pete did not know what had gone wrong, but he did know that Julian was demonstrating all the body language of anger, so he cowered down. Julian grabbed hold of Pete by the scruff of his neck, dragged him across the floor; pushed his nose against the damaged chair legs; and started to whack his bottom with heavy smacks. Pete squirmed partly in pain, but more in heartache because he did not know what had gone wrong. Julian kept shouting, 'You know what you've done!' Pete did not know what he'd done, all he had done out of boredom was chew a chair leg.

He didn't understand why somebody he had regarded as a friend, was now so angry, and so hurtful. That evening, Peter had no dinner.

You naughty dog

Next morning, Julian fed Pete and left for work. His mother—who had paid for the chairs—did come in and take him for a walk, but kept saying, 'You naughty dog'. Other than the fact that she was angry, Pete did not know what being a naughty dog meant, nor why he was being criticised. The friend was a bit later than usual in coming in, which at least shortened the afternoon, but Pete was still bored with nothing to do, and had another go at the chair leg.

Again, Pete was delighted to hear Julian coming back up the stairs, and again stood eagerly at the slit of the door. Julian started to fondle Pete when he saw the increased damage to the chair. He went ballistic. Again, Pete was dragged across the floor, had his nose banged against the chair leg, and was then dragged down the stairs to the garage, into which he was thrown for the rest of the night. Pete just did not know what he had done wrong other than amusing himself while waiting for Julian. He knew Julian was angry but he did not know why he had had another beating and been dragged into the garage without a meal. His backside throbbed with pain. He was upset that Julian was upset and longed for his company. He was cold, there was a terrific draught coming in under the door of the garage, he had no bed and no shelter other than trying to crawl behind some boxes in the corner.

When Julian came down in the morning, he had Pete's breakfast and threw his bed into one of the corners before taking Pete for the briefest of walks. His mother did come, but with very bad grace, and gave him the briefest of walks. Pete was heartbroken. He was cold, he was hungry, he had barely had enough time to relieve himself properly, the wind was still howling under the door, and he had had no affection from Julian or his mother.

48

He started whimpering with grief. The colder he got, the louder his whimpers became. Some of the other tenants of the flats had heard Pete being punished, and had seen him being dragged down the steps to the garage. They realised how cold he would be, and had heard him crying piteously all morning. They started talking to each other, expressing their concerns. For a change, the lunch time friend was early. It transpired that he was not really a friend but merely a neighbour who was trying to be helpful. When he arrived, some of the other neighbours saw him and came down to express their concern.

By then, Pete was a shivering wreck pathetically grateful for the care and attention he was now receiving. The 'friend' took Pete back to his own house, laid him in front of the fire, and gave him some food. In the meantime, one of the neighbours had rung the RSPCA who came quite quickly and took Pete away with them, leaving a note for Julian. So, Pete found himself in a nice warm kennel, with a proper bed, receiving treatment from a vet, and with the care and compassion of a kennel maid.

When Julian got home that evening, an RSPCA inspector was waiting to interview him and to give him a formal warning of his unacceptable conduct.

Kennel life

While Pete was comforted by the feeling that he was in a 'cocoon' of care, he was still in pain from his smackings and still heartbroken that his one-time friend, Julian, had turned against him. Over time his pains eased, the care and concern of his kennel maid was a great comfort, and it was interesting to be able to see and talk to the dogs in the other kennels.

The daily parade

Initially, Pete did not realise what was happening when there was a parade of humans past his kennel, nor why some of his kennel mates were looking so eager, wagging their tails, and trying to kiss some of the fingers put through the wire netting of the cages. His neighbour, another collie, explained that the humans were looking at the dogs with a view to taking one home with them, while the dogs were trying to make sure that they were the one to be chosen.

Pete was so morose that nobody paid any attention to him but as he improved, he started to take more interest. He, too, went up to the wire, sparkled his eyes, wagged his tail, and looked eagerly at every human, wondering which one might choose him, and whether or not they looked the type who would be kind and caring. Like all the other inhabitants, he stood with his tail gradually drooping with disappointment when he was disregarded, though he was always pleased to see the happiness of a dog which had been chosen.

Heartbreak

Gradually, Pete started to regain his spirits. The daily grooming by his kennel maid restored the gloss of his coat. He started to smile at people and kiss their hands through the netting more eagerly. Eventually, a handsome, smartly-dressed man with charming manners who was saying all the right things, in the right way, came and stood by his run. Like my first owner, Helen, all the kennel staff were particularly taken by how handsome and considerate he was being. But Pete was appalled. The man was his first owner!

The friendly character who was good fun to be with, was also a character who could equally be totally unreasonable and had ended up by throwing hot fat all over Pete. Pete did not know what to do. His instinct, as with most of us dogs, was to go up and be friendly and to show his affection for the good days, while on the other hand, he could not stop thinking about the terribly bad days he had experienced at the hands of the man now beaming at him.

The kennel staff were so enamoured with this charming man that they bent over backwards to help him take Pete up the corridor, and into his car. The kennel maid who had been particularly fond of Pete was somewhat concerned by Pete's attitude towards the man, and knew him well enough to think there must be something not quite right. She too was carried away by the general enthusiasm. But, as Pete looked back at her from the car taking him away, he sensed that she was upset and worried on his behalf. We dogs live in the present, in the here and now, we don't dwell on what could happen, or what has happened, but Pete could not avoid wondering how and why his former owner had reappeared in his life.

Kind character

Initially, all went well. The man was in one of his 'good' moods, was friendly, took Pete on regular walks, played with him in the garden, and fed him on a regular basis. So, Pete started to relax and feel happy.

Unfriendly character

Then, when Pete woke up one morning, he realised, to his horror that the man had switched back into being the deeply-depressed, angry and violent individual, sweeping dishes off the table and seeking an outlet for his anger. Pete tried to find somewhere to hide. All the doors were shut so his options were limited. All he could do was to hide behind the coal scuttle.

Then the man's mood appeared to have changed. He whistled to Pete and took him out to the car as if they were going out to drive somewhere for a walk. While Pete became less fearful, he was not entirely reassured. Though the man seemed to be trying to appear to be normal, Pete sensed that there was an ominous falseness to his actions.

After some time, the car stopped, and the man whistled

to Pete to come out of the car, and go for a walk. The walk did not last for very long before the man called Pete to him, tied a piece of string around his collar, and tied him quite tightly against a pillar before driving off. Pete was most uncomfortable, he could just about sit up, there was no way in which he could lie down. If he did try to lie down, his collar cut into his neck. There was no access to water. There was nothing to eat.

Seven long days

Pete hoped that the man would return. In his earlier time with this man, Pete had often been tied by short lead in an outhouse, but was always eventually released. Pete hoped that the same thing would happen again, that the man would return and release him. But, he didn't.

Pete spent seven long days tied to that post. Seven days of hell. He tried to stand up to ease the pressure on his neck and to pass his motions. He tried to sit down, but when it rained, his collar tightened. Then, on the seventh day, some workmen appeared. They were horrified at his appearance. He had had no water to drink, no food to eat. His neck was raw. He looked a virtual skeleton. Hurriedly, the men released him, gently helped him to lie down and gave him a small amount of water. They weren't experts, and were worried that if they gave him too much too soon, it might do more harm than good. One workman had a mobile phone, and he dialled 999 for the police. When he explained the situation, they said they would come, and would bring a vet.

Everyone at the scene was heartbroken by the appalling cruelty and desperate to do something to help but the vet came to the conclusion that it would be much kinder to put him to sleep.

Pete was still wearing the collar he had been given at the rescue centre, so this enabled the police to track down his owner who admitted that he had left Pete exactly one week before he was found. The RSPCA inspector said it was unthinkable how much pain Pete must have been in during the seven days he was left with no food or water, and left outdoors, exposed to the freezing winter weather.

It makes me feel sick and heartbroken to have to tell you this story.

Rampant unkindness

While Pete's story was particularly upsetting, we dogs are appalled at the random unkindness that so many dog owners inflict on us.

One of the walks which my dad and mum and I enjoyed was to go from Broadsands beach and walk across the downs to Elberry. This is a very popular walk where you can see dogs thoroughly enjoying themselves running around, saying hello to passing dogs, and responding to their owners who are throwing balls for them. But, over the years, I witnessed quite a few incidents which gave me cause for concern, so let me tell you about just three examples.

A peaceful walk!

While I, and most of the other dogs, were running free on Broadsands beach, we once passed a young collie pulling at quite a short lead, desperate to join in the fun. We heard the woman in the group exclaiming with total frustration, 'I thought we were out for a nice, peaceful walk'.

I ask you, if they took a young boy, or a young girl, out for a play, wouldn't they want to run around, playing games and enjoying themselves? So why should they expect a young puppy to be any different? Clearly, the young pup wanted to be able to enjoy himself, to run, to play. If they were worried he was not yet fully trained, then he could have been put on one of the leads which expand and retract. I think my dad, my mum and I all felt that the days of that pup were likely to be numbered if his owners could not recognise that a young dog, like a young human, needs to play.

Total idiocy

On another occasion, we had watched a man proudly demonstrating the use of his 'soundless whistle' to which his dog had been responding promptly. But when he returned to his owner, he had promptly started bellowing at him. How idiotic can a human get?

One moment he has a dog responding to silent whistles, and the next he is deafening the dog by shouting at him in a way which totally confuses it. In fact, the dog was so confused he wasn't sure whether to stay, or go, or come, or what he should do. Reluctantly, his inherent doggie desire to please took over, and he did approach the man, only to receive a vicious swipe across the face, following which the man bellowed, 'That will teach you to come when you're told!'

Would a human approach a ruffian likely to swipe them viciously across the face? How stupid can humans get. In fact, several times we saw dogs being punished for not coming when called. I repeat, would humans want to approach somebody whose idea of 'motivation' was to inflict pain? Humans like to approach people who are kind and friendly. Why should dogs be any different. Surely humans have enough sense to find ways of motivating and rewarding dogs which come when told, and are greeted warmly for having done so.

Unimaginable cruelty

My final story relates to the day we met a very attractive young collie bitch who only had three legs. Obviously, I immediately asked her what had happened, and my owners asked the same question of the man who was now her owner.

It transpired that her original owner had no understanding of how to train a dog. Being quite young, when she had been let off the lead, she frisked around, played with the other dogs and generally enjoyed herself, much to the frustration of her owner who could not get her to come back. He had tried chasing after her, but she thought that was a lovely game, and played hide and seek with him. Eventually, now being almost apoplectic with anger and frustration, he caught hold of her by one of her legs, and spun her around in the air before letting her fly off into a bank of blackberry bushes. While his dog struggled and screamed pitifully, he stamped off in anger.

Concerned bystanders, attracted the attention of a park attendant on a tractor with a container at the back. He reversed his tractor and its container into the bushes to the point where he could extract the bitch, who was then rushed by one of the bystanders to the nearest vet. I didn't understand what had happened to the owner, but the attractive young bitch now looked well cared for and seemed to be able to enjoy life, despite having lost one of her legs.

Conclusion

Quite obviously, from the number of dogs we see on our walks across to Elberry, there are a lot of loving owners, providing a very happy life to their pets. But, quite clearly, there is also an undercurrent of owners who do not understand dogs, do not know how to treat them, and all too often, are extremely unkind if not downright cruel to the dogs in their care.

Chapter Seven

Happy's six homes

Stability vital

Dogs need stability. They need a 'leader' prepared to ensure a stable environment. If a human cannot provide this stability, then the dog or dogs of the human concerned will be unsettled and may even try to take over as the pack leader.

A close relationship

I have been very lucky. My dad and mum have a very close relationship where each tries to please and help the other with seldom a cross word passing between them, and certainly very few upsets.

There was one, some years ago, when Mum was very upset and tearful about the illness of a much-loved friend. Dad was trying to comfort her by giving her a cuddle. I circled around them, trying to find some way of helping. In the end, I squeezed between their legs and stood between them, looking up, trying to convey my love and concern. Mum immediately went down, gave my ears an initial tickle, and then gave me a cuddle while Dad made a cup of tea. As I say, I was very lucky to have such a stable relationship.

My sister Happy

My sister, Happy, was not so lucky. She had been chosen by what seemed to be a very nice couple who had told our initial owner, Helen, that they were buying a dog because they could not have the children they had wanted. In fact, I remember my real mother, Jess, showing her concern about this, and asking herself the question, what will happen if and when they do have children? But, initially, all went well. Every weekday the husband disappeared to 'go to work'. Happy could not really understand what he did, nor where he did it, but he seemed to disappear quite often. So, Happy spent all her time with the wife who was keen to do all the right things.

Toilet training

The first thing the wife did was to be very sympathetic towards Happy as far as toilet training was concerned. She got up early to give Happy her first walk and throughout the day took her out into the garden for regular opportunities for going to the toilet. She took her for her last walk as late as possible, and provided a pile of newspapers in case Happy had an accident during the night. As a result, Happy, like me, very quickly learned how to 'be clean'.

Wife's Baby

The wife had been told by her vet about the importance of teaching Happy how to relate with other dogs, and with other humans, and how to cope with the everyday activities of humans, which we dogs need to understand and adjust to. The wife took her to puppy classes, which Happy found great fun and helped her to build relationships with other dogs. The wife was obviously very frustrated by her inability to have children, so Happy became her 'baby', and went with her on regular walks, out in the car with her, and was always close to her in the house. In fact, Happy got the distinct feeling that the husband was somewhat jealous of the attention she received from the wife, who seemed to be more concerned to tell him about how brilliant Happy was than listening to him talking.

Pregnant

Then, perhaps because of all the 'motherly love' the wife had been lavishing on Happy, she became pregnant. Happy didn't really understand what was happening but somehow the wife seemed to become even closer and while Happy did not understand what the wife was saying, she seemed to be sharing something important with her.

Happy sensed that the husband was getting even more fed up. He could barely be bothered to have anything to do with Happy and started nudging her out of the way, and even shutting Happy in the kitchen to exclude her from her close involvement with his wife. Happy did not really understand what was going on, but heard the wife telling her husband that the vet had spoken about the importance of not creating jealousy between Happy and the new baby. Happy got the distinct impression that this made the husband even more cross and bad tempered.

Happy and the baby

Happy was happy when her owner took her into the bedroom, laid her new baby on a clean sheet on the floor and put Happy on a loose lead to allow her to investigate the new arrival. Once her curiosity had been satisfied, Happy was given a titbit and a short walk. Thereafter, the wife followed a similar routine of letting Happy inspect her new baby and then giving her a titbit and a short outing.

Husband's anger

The husband became furious at the concern his wife was showing to ensure that Happy was not jealous of the new arrival. Happy heard him shouting that now that they had their long-awaited baby, she—it was a girl—should take precedence and Happy should 'like it or lump it'. In fact, what should have been a very happy occasion with the arrival of their daughter, became a bone of contention with the husband's long-simmering resentment of Happy boiling up into outright anger. He felt that now they had their baby, Happy should be relegated into being a 'normal dog'.

A terrible day

While the husband was increasingly resentfully, his wife continued to treat Happy as very much 'part of the family', even though she was relegated to the kitchen whenever the husband came home. One Saturday, the husband arrived home unexpectedly early. He found his wife giving their baby a cuddle with Happy snuggling against his wife, and giving their baby a friendly lick whenever she could.

The husband exploded with anger. Happy was frightened and started to run down the passage, which led to the stairs, but the husband caught up with her and kicked her down the stairs in a fit of rage. She tried to regain her balance but ended up rolling, head over heels, down the final set of stairs where she lay, whimpering, partly because her jaw hurt, and partly because of what the husband might do next.

Without pause, the husband put her into his car and drove down to the vets to ask them for the address of the nearest 'rescue home'. Wisely, the vet asked to see Happy; gave her an examination, and told the husband that she had bruises on her jaw and in her ribs. Somewhat reluctantly, the owner agreed to meet the cost of the care needed, but made it plain that because 'his wife could not cope', Happy would need to be re-homed.

Rescue home

So, once she recovered, Happy ended up in a rescue centre. Having been used to living in a very nice home, she found the transition into a wired enclosure difficult to comprehend. The kennel staff was marvellous, and did their best to show affection, and the dogs in the adjoining runs did their best to be friendly. But, all Happy wanted to do, was to curl up in a ball and whimper softly to herself.

New home

Eventually, Happy was found a new home which should have been the start of a new and happy life for her, but this was not to be.

Her new home was with a lady who also owned two German shepherds. Both dogs relentlessly bullied Happy and wouldn't even allow her to get into the garden to go to the toilet. While she did her best to get into a corner of the garden, more often than not she could only go in the house. As soon as she saw the mess, the owner would grab Happy by the scruff of her neck and rub her nose in the mess 'to teach her a lesson'. As I said earlier, would a human rub her baby's nose in a soiled nappy to teach the baby a lesson? We dogs think humans are so odd. However, the woman found looking after Happy too much of a nuisance so she was, once again, put into a rescue centre.

Farmer's wife

Her third owner was the widow of a farmer, who had had a great deal to do with the collies on the farm, so she seemed an ideal owner. The widow quickly came to adore Happy and helped her to regain her confidence. The widow knew that, as a collie, she needed plenty of exercise and so took her for regular walks, which gave her the chance to stop and talk to the other dog owners she met and also gave Happy the chance to make friends with the dogs she met.

Happy started to feel really happy and to become really fond of her new owner. Then tragedy struck. The widow fell awkwardly, which aggravated the problems she was already experiencing with her hips. She found it difficult to take Happy for her normal walks. Instead, knowing how important regular walks were for a collie, she arranged for a neighbour's daughter to give Happy three good walks a day, in the morning, the early afternoon when she got back from work, and in the evening. In between these walks, the widow could potter into the garden with Happy.

The final straw

One of the walks took them on a bridge over a stream. The walls of the bridge were not that high, and Happy created a game of trotting along the top of the bridge and smiling at the daughter who would often respond by playfully cuffing her ears. It was a harmless enough game but one which added to their enjoyment of the walk.

One day, there were some teenagers on the bridge who, when Happy went to walk past them, pushed her into the stream. Fortunately, the water was high enough to cushion her fall so she swam to the bank, walked up the rather muddy banks and trotted back to the daughter who was still standing on the bridge rather shocked by what had happened. As Happy came toward her, one of the boys picked her up again, and threw her in the water for a second time. This made Happy very worried and unhappy and she scooted past the boys to get well away from them. The daughter had to run after her. Obviously, Happy was wet and bedraggled while the daughter was tearful at her failure to protect Happy from the teenagers. Understandably, the widow was upset for both of them.

This was the final straw for the widow. She realised she was too old, and too infirm, to be able to care for Happy in the way that she should, and, very reluctantly, tearfully, she sent Happy back to the rescue centre.

Rescue centre again

So, poor Happy found herself back in the kennels. Again, the staff tried to do their best to comfort her as did the dogs on each side of her kennel, but Happy was really upset. She had begun to get really fond of the widow and enjoyed being taken out by the neighbour's daughter, but at least she knew how to settle into the routine of the kennels.

Heartbreak

Gradually, Happy started to regain her spirits. The daily grooming by her kennel maid restored the gloss of her coat. She started to smile at people and kiss their hands more eagerly. Eventually, success! She was chosen by what seemed to be a very nice, middle-aged couple. Though she was sorry to leave her kennel maid, who had given her so much love, and sad to leave the friends she had made in adjoining kennels, she was up on her toes to be taken out of her kennel, along the passage, and lifted into their car. Joy of joys, her life was getting back to normal. She watched with eagerness as the car drove her to their home.

The elderly lady she had loved so much, had been very house proud, and taught her how to behave in the house. So, she was very good, very polite, and, while keen to investigate her new home, lay down when told. But, even when lying down, Happy could not suppress her submerged energy. Her head was up, her eyes were bright, her whole body was geared for action and her tail twitched in keenness after the inevitable frustration of kennel life. She had been taken out into the garden and had been able to go to the toilet but this had not eased her restlessness.

After lunch, she was put into their car and taken down to a large park. Initially, she had been kept on a lead. Again, the farmer's widow had trained her to walk to heel, so this was not a problem. Then, she was let off the lead. The spring of energy within her exploded. She took off, and sprinted away like a rocket to the far end of the park. Her potential owners were worried sick that she was running away. In fact, when she got to the end of the park, she turned around and sprinted fast as ever back to them, dancing with relief, and bounding around them with a broad grin, really happy to be with them, and start being a real collie again.

Two intense

She could not understand why her prospective owners did not return her smiles and no longer seemed quite so affectionate. However, she was quite happy to bounce back into their car to be taken home, except that she was not taken home. She was taken back to the kennels she had left that morning. The prospective owners told the staff on duty that Happy was 'far too intense for them'. They said she was like a coiled spring waiting to explode, as indeed she had done, when sprinting across the park.

Given how well she had behaved in their house, and when on a lead, Happy could really not understand why she had been rejected. Her kennel maid gave her a lovely long hug and her friends nuzzled her through the wire of their runs, but she whimpered quietly to herself as she curled up in the corner of her run.

Warning bells

After being rejected, it was almost as if warning bells sounded to humans who came to look at Happy. It may have been the subconscious attitudes of the staff, who are well aware that they have to handle an increasing number of collies who have been rejected because they are far too intense. Collies are workaholics who enjoy the physical nature of their work and the intellectual stimulus involved in controlling a flock of sheep, and many do not adjust to a far less interesting life as a pet.

Hurtfulness of rejection

Once, when I was listening to a group of humans talking, I gathered that they were saying how hurtful it was for a human to be rejected. I remember thinking to myself that it is just as hurtful for a dog to be rejected. The fact that she had now been rejected three times did not make it any easier for Happy to bear. Certainly, it was great to see the kennel maids, one of whom was always very loving to her, and it was great to talk to the other collies desperately waiting for a new home, but still to be rejected, was hard to bear.

This time, she did not have long to wait. The kennel maid had been giving her regular brushings so Happy looked really fit and responded quickly when what seemed to be a very nice couple stopped to take an interest in her. Happy could not stop herself, she smiled at them, tried to lick their fingers between the wires of her run; and wagged her tail vigorously. Clearly, the humans were very interested. Happy was a bit worried by the way in which her kennel maid seemed to be not quite so keen, as if she had some reservations about their suitability to take Happy away with them. Happy heard her saying that 'they seemed too glib'. She wasn't too sure what this meant but it did not sound good.

A family from hell

When they were talking to the staff from the rescue centre, the couple interested in Happy explained that they had a 'grown-up family'. What they did not say was several members of their 'grown-up' family still lived with them, and into the bargain, had children of their own who were living with them too, so Happy found herself taken into a home of absolute bedlam. Children were racing around, fighting, or certainly arguing, with each other. Some of the older children had music blaring away. The couple who had gone to the rescue centre in smart clothes to impress, quickly changed into very casual clothing and took absolutely no notice of what their children or grandchildren were doing. They certainly made no effort to control them, their activities, or the noise they were making. Happy was not only deafened by the noise, she was totally confused by all the conflicting activities and by the total lack of any evidence of a 'pack leader'. No-one was in charge. It was total bedlam.

The door to the back garden was open, so Happy escaped into the garden and hid herself in the far corner, under some bushes. Eventually, one of the granddaughters came to find her and sat down with Happy, giving her a very pleasant stroke and cuddle. As a result, she was able to entice Happy into going indoors for her dinner. At first, Happy was alone with the granddaughter and, being hungry, started to eat her meal but, before she had got very far, the doors crashed open and some of the other grandchildren and their parents came in, so bedlam was created once more. Happy was desperate to find some peace. To escape the noise, she made her way upstairs, going up until she got away from the noise, which she achieved by going right up into the attic where the granddaughter found her again and kept her company. However, it was not long before the grandchildren started coming upstairs to go to bed so bedlam reigned once more.

Taking charge

Our forbears, the wolves, could not function without a strong, unchallenged, pack leader. Similarly, we dogs cannot function without a strong, unchallenged pack leader. As happens quite often, where the humans are unable or unwilling to act as the pack leader, the most senior dog in the family will decide that he has to do so. Normally, it is a male dog who will take action, but, as the only dog in the house, Happy felt that she had to do something to create some order if she was to avoid being driven mad by the chaos.

The basic instinct of any collie is to 'round up' the flock. So, Happy started to round up the parents, the grandparents, and the children, nipping their heels if necessary, to get them to do what she wanted. Every member of the family thought that Happy had gone mad. Some shut themselves in their room; some ran out of the doors; a few even jumped out of the windows. Happy ended up sitting by herself, in the living room. It was certainly quiet without the family, but it was not what Happy had intended.

Police called

The outcome of Happy's efforts to restore order was that the police were informed and they asked the RSPCA inspector to look into the matter, who in turn, asked a friend of his, who was a vet, to go with him. The vet knew the family because he had been asked to destroy one of their previous dogs. The RSPCA inspector and the vet, quickly realised the situation. Happy was sitting unhappily in the lounge and was very pleased to see the vet and the inspector arrive. In fact, she hoped that one of them would take over as pack leader and achieve the rational behaviour, as she had been trying to do. The police asked that Happy should be destroyed but the vet asked for time to investigate further, given his previous knowledge of the family.

So, Happy was taken back to the kennels at the familiar rescue centre while the vet made his enquiries. He rang all his veterinary colleagues in the area asking if they had dealt with this family and he also rang all the rescue centres in the area to find out if they had any knowledge of them. As a result, it transpired that over the years, this family had taken in six dogs, often very young puppies, and then had given them back to the same or a different rescue centre, or asked a vet to put them down for being 'dangerous'. Privately, the vet felt that the family concerned should be prosecuted for their cruelty but he was able to persuade the police, and the family, that he should be allowed to find a good home for Happy.

This request was reinforced when the kennel maid from the refuge centre, who had looked after Happy whenever she was at the centre, agreed that she would take Happy home. Apparently, the kennel maid had fallen in love with Happy and had a husband who was a long-distance runner so they felt that he could provide Happy with the exercise she needed by taking her with him on his runs.

Home at last

So, one morning, Happy was surprised to see her kennel maid calling to collect her on her day off with her tall, handsome husband. Proudly, Happy went up on her toes, her ears went up, her eyes sparkled, she was smiling at everyone she passed, but her tail still wagged sedately as she walked, nicely to heel, down the passage of the kennels for the last time. Stability was back in her life.

Chapter Eight

Clever Clogs's enjoyable life

Obedience and agility training

Some years ago my dad and mum drove me to the far side of Plymouth and eventually drove into a field where some form of dog training activities seemed to be going on. The lady doing the training eventually came over to us and took us to an area which had a sequence of different obstacles. Later, I realised that it was what was called an 'agility course'. I gathered that the lady was saying that it took time to train a dog to go around the course but, very quietly, my dad asked if perhaps he could put me around it.

I forget the precise sequence now, but I remember one obstacle was quite a high sheet of thick wood leaning at quite a sharp angle against another similar sheet of wood forming a 'V'. Dad gave me a quiet command of 'up' and a hand signal waving me up, but when I got to the top he whispered 'stay' and he then gave a hand signal that I should go down the other side. It was a bit of a surprise but it was fun. I remember another obstacle involved my going up a plank which went up to the top of some bricks with another much longer plank of wood going along, in mid air, to another pile of bricks where there was a plank going down the other side. Again, initially a bit disconcerting, but fun.

I have always loved jumping, so it was easy to jump over a gate, and to jump through a line of tyres. I cannot remember all the obstacles, but my only problem was when confronted by an opening leading into what was obviously a tunnel. Dad took me to one side to show me that though the sacking had collapsed along the middle of the tunnel, there was an exit where my mum was standing. After a bit of hesitation, I got the idea that I was meant to go through the tunnel to my mum, but since this involved pushing against the area where the sacking was sagging down, I had to think twice before pushing my way through to emerge to a hug from my mum.

I was really switched on and excited and, of my own accord, went around a number of the obstacles for a second time, particularly the jumps. The dog trainer was very impressed. Sadly, visiting the training centre was over a 100-mile trip there and back, so it was not realistic to go on a regular basis.

Clever Clogs

However, one of my sisters was lucky. The lovely lady who had given her such a thorough examination when we were still with Helen, was a dog trainer who had bought Clever Clogs to add to her team of highly-trained dogs which gave regular displays at various shows in aid of charity, but more seriously took part in agility competitions.

Going to a show

Once, my dad and mum took me to an agricultural show because they had seen that there was going to be a dog display. When we got there, there was a group of ladies with their dogs waiting to give their demonstration. I quickly recognised Clever Clogs while my dad and mum recognised the lady they had met when she was thinking about buying her. So, while the humans were talking to each other, I had a chance to talk to my sister.

Initially, she had been taught how to behave in very gentle, quite short periods of what were almost games. In fact, my sister said it was fun, particularly as she was always rewarded when she did what was expected of her in the right way. Her prize was always a titbit. We didn't have much time because her mistress called her to heel to get ready for the demonstration. All my sister could do was to tell me to make sure that I watched her during the performance.

Obedience display

There was a team of eight dogs, all collies, which gave a wonderful display. It started when the dogs and their owners walked in a figure of eight so they crossed each other in the middle, with the dogs keeping very close to their owner and paying no attention to the dog they were passing.

Then they would walk in-line abreast and as their owners said 'sit—stay', all eight dogs sat down immediately in a perfect line abreast. The owners did a walk around and came back behind their dogs and, as they reached them, they said 'heel', and all eight dogs got up and again walked in line abreast with their owners. All the dogs were then told to lie down and again, they all did it at the same time to remain in line abreast. Then they were told to stay and again their owners walked around behind them, stopped, and gave them a smile and a stroke at the end of the exercises.

Again, it is difficult for me to remember, but a demonstration was also given on the retrieve. A dog would sit while a dumbbell was thrown some way ahead, and then went to collect it, return, sit in front of his owner, gently put the dumbbell into her hand, and then go round the back of his owner to sit by her side in the heel position. When the display was over, all the dogs bounded around, tails wagging, pleased as punch with themselves, and obviously thrilled to be working as a team with their owners, giving a display which had given so much pleasure to all those watching.

Agility competition

A bit later in the day, we watched Clever Clogs and her team mates taking part in an agility competition. I really envied their ability to have so much fun. We collies can really sprint very fast, so I felt very sorry for her owner having to run around the obstacles with her.

Quite obviously, Clever Clogs was really enjoying herself because she was replicating what she would do as a collie; sprinting around to collect and control her sheep. When she had finished her circuit, I could see that Clever Clogs was dancing around with joy and the satisfaction of receiving a broad smile and a cuddle from her owner. I thought to myself that it is a pity that more owners of collies do not give their dog the chance to join in activities of this type.

Chapter Nine

The Boss – A real working collie

Envy

While I have had a wonderful life, I must admit I felt a tinge of envy when I heard that my eldest brother – the one we called 'The Boss' as puppies – had been chosen by a nearby farmer to be trained as a working sheepdog.

Learning to be a sheep dog

I learned on 'the grapevine' that he had enjoyed his initial training. Twice a day the farmer would take him into a field and – with a gentle patience – school him to appreciate what was expected of him. Near the farm buildings there was a large, circular enclosure, used for the sheep. My brother was taken to this and trained to 'go round'. Once he had got used to this, he thoroughly enjoyed obeying this command. However, what he really enjoyed was going out in the fields and learning how to control the sheep.

Leadership

The farmer was very much the leader of a team of six collies, of which my brother was the most junior. He was puzzled. He could not understand how the farmer could control six dogs at once. Eventually he realised the work of herding sheep was so physically demanding that the shepherd would often use the dogs in pairs; using one pair in the morning, and the other pair in the afternoon, and would use different sets of dogs according to their particular skills.

However, there were occasions when the entire flock was being moved, when all six dogs were needed. These dogs were given their commands by a special whistle and each dog was trained to react just to his or her own particular set of whistles. Initially my brother found this disconcerting but the shepherd was very clever and always used the right whistle in the right way for the right dog.

Sorting the sheep

Apparently, the farming year started in the autumn when the flock had to be sorted into the ewes that were going to be used for breeding and those which were going for mutton. This involved bringing the flock into central pens, sorting them, and splitting them into different groups going to different fields, according to the quality of the feed in each field.

The rams

Then came an exciting time. They had to fetch in the rams, big, ugly awkward brutes, only too keen to fight each other and to try to vent their spleen on the dogs trying to get them into the relevant pen. Apart from being given a general examination and tidy up, the main reason for this was to enable the shepherd to fit a harness to each ram, which held a coloured marker between the ram's forelegs. This meant that when the ram mated with a sheep, the farmer could see by the colour of the marker which members of the flock had been served. My brother said it was quite dangerous to control the rams when they were in the pens. They were only too keen to turn on the dogs if they could.

My brother was once cornered by a ram, which put his head down and tried to butt him with all his strength. Had he connected, his ribs could have been crushed. Fortunately, he had the sense to drop down on his tummy and scoot out from under, but it was a very lucky escape.

Empathy

My brother explained that a good dog needs brains and vision to reason his way around the situations he finds himself in. Most importantly, a dog needs to develop an empathy with his shepherd so that even when they are some way apart, they can 'communicate' by small signals and body language. Apparently, one important tool for a working collie is his eyesight. Not only does a dog have tremendous vision at long range, but once we were called Eye Dogs because we can give particularly piercing looks, vital when facing down a sheep, and also invaluable in terms of communicating the intensity of our feelings to our shepherd.

Sixth sense

Once, my brother said, he had been herding sheep out of a field where the banks were overgrown with thick brambles.

The rounding up was going quite well until his sixth sense told him that something was wrong. Perhaps, despite the noise of the lambs being gathered, he had picked up a bleat, or just some instinct, or a little tuft of wool or a muddy hoof mark in the wrong place, but he jumped up onto the bank and saw a lamb with its thick woollen coat trapped in a mass of brambles. He jumped down off the bank, and ran a few yards towards his shepherd at the far side of the field. Once he was sure that the shepherd was looking at him he jumped back up onto the top of the bank, looked down at the lamb, and then gave his shepherd 'the eye' look. When he had first disappeared, he had jumped down to have a closer inspection and tried to pull the lamb out by himself. It was when his efforts had failed that he jumped back up on the wall to signal to his shepherd.

His shepherd trusted him, knew that he was giving him a signal to find help, and went across to rescue the lamb. Proudly, my brother said that while a good dog has to understand a shepherd, a good shepherd has to learn to have the empathy and to understand his dogs.

Saving the day

I often saw my brother at work and once he told me another story.

The shepherd had used two of the other dogs to drive part of the flock into a group of fields he had rented from a local farmer, but he took my brother with him to collect the flock and bring them back home. The shepherd was puzzled; there were no sheep in the first field, no sheep in the second field, and then—worry of worry—no sheep in the third field! Apparently, my brother saved the day, though he had never been in the fields before, he worked out what had happened. His first clue was that there was a place where there was mud on the wall and as he approached, he started to hear the bleats of lambs so he jumped over the wall and found the flock. He then rounded them up and drove them towards the point in the wall where they had jumped over.

His shepherd was very pleased to see a line of lambs jumping back over the wall so they could be driven home. My brother was justifiably proud of himself in solving the problem, so that when he caught up with the shepherd, he gave him a cheerful grin and tail wag, while the shepherd returned his grin with a broad smile, a softly spoken, 'Well done', and a quick pat. He was really elated by the close partnership of the moment. It made him feel that his life was really worthwhile.

Another time my brother told me about was the time he went out with a bitch called Maisie to check on the sheep grazing a headland field, when his shepherd was approached by a walker saying that a sheep had fallen down the cliff. When the shepherd and the two dogs got to the spot, in some ways it was not as bad as it sounded. The sheep with her lamb had not fallen down the cliff, she had just made her way down a very narrow path. Nonetheless, it was going to be very difficult to retrieve her.

To his chagrin, the shepherd thought that my brother was probably too intense to handle the problem. Instead, he used Maisie, who was lighter, smaller, perhaps more nimble and less frightening. Maisie was fantastic, she listened to the almost whispered commands she received, and got herself in a position behind the sheep and the lamb while the shepherd worked his way down to the point where he could use his curved crop, which was long enough to loop around the sheep, and pull it into his arms. My brother said it was a bit of a struggle for the shepherd to carry the sheep up the narrow path but he got her to the cliff top and once her lamb had caught her up, she trotted off happily. This time it was Maisie who got a quiet, 'Well done', a smile and a pat.

Sorting the sheep

One thing which did intrigue me was the way in which the sheep, once they had become pregnant, were brought back to the farm prior to their giving birth. They were put through a machine—I think it was called a scanner—which told the shepherd whether the ewe was just going to have one lamb, or two or three. Those having multiple births were left in the sheds, while those only having a single birth were taken back to the fields. It was all a bit beyond me.

One of the things that sounded very dangerous was that when the sheep were in the shed, they had to be fed by dropping a big bale of hay into their racks. But, sheep are stupid animals, and if they got too close to the racks too soon, they could be killed as the bale dropped down on them. So, my brother and his friends took it in turns to patrol the racks and keep the sheep out of harms way whenever a bale had to be dropped.

Quad bikes

One day when walking past the farm, I had seen quad bikes hurtling by with two or three lucky sheepdogs on the back, wagging their tales with exhilaration, so it was no surprise to me when my brother said how much he enjoyed going out on the quad bike. Sometimes, they went out to fill the troughs out in the fields with meal, but what he liked better was when they did a tour of inspection making sure all the sheep and lambs were healthy. If they were not, and it was usually the lambs rather than the sheep with a problem, the lamb would have to be separated from its mother so that the shepherd could give it the right attention.

My brother said that separating a lamb away from its mother in a large field was tremendous fun and he felt great when he succeeded in getting the lamb close enough to the shepherd for treatment. Once, one of the lambs could not stand properly so he and one of his mates, another sheepdog, had to stand on each side of the lamb to keep it upright until it could be treated. I thought that was very clever for the two dogs to work together.

My regret

While I was looking forward to going to live with my new owners, I must admit that I felt a sense of regret that I had not been chosen to become a sheepdog like The Boss, who I felt was very lucky. He would have the physical exhilaration of being able to run, flat out, to gather the sheep and then the sheer challenge of driving the sheep, who may not always want to go where they were told. It seems a big word for me, but he would have the sheer intellectual satisfaction of being able to use his brains to think through solutions to the problems he met. He would be a valued member of a team of six dogs, all of whom interacted well together and, in particular, were able to work in partnership with each other.

Bond with shepherd

Finally, he would have a relationship with his shepherd, a great empathy and understanding, have the thrill of working with and for his shepherd and—above all—have the satisfaction of being praised and rewarded for a job well done.

This type of excitement, the challenge, the sheer physical thrill of covering 20, 30, even 40 miles a day, not being told what to do, but anticipating what needs to be done even before the shepherd realises that there is a problem, creates a deep-seated bond with his shepherd. Collies really feel needed and valued, and in return, give total love, instinct, intelligence, physical dexterity and stamina.

Buying a collie

It made me think that anyone considering buying a collie as a pet, should think seriously about whether they will be able to provide these qualities to the puppy they might buy. I almost feel like saying that nobody should buy a genuine working collie as a pet, but then I realised that I had been bought as a pet and had had a wonderful life.

PART TWO

Chapter Ten

Learning how to behave

Initial home

Once all my brothers and sisters had left, I moved in with my mother to stay in the home Helen shared with her three daughters. They were only too keen to play with me, and take me for short walks.

My mother's help

I was particularly pleased to be staying with my mother. When she was worried about losing her pups she had been really upset. By herself and with me, she relaxed and became the loving mother I had first known. While she did not hesitate to teach me how to behave, it was done in a really gentle, loving way. Often she would go for a walk around the farm and teach me to keep close to her, though I must admit that I did dance around her in sheer happiness.

Helen's vet

While I was still quite young, a handsome man came to see us. In fact, he gave each of my brothers and sisters and I a cuddle. Trouble was that while giving me 'a cuddle', I felt a sharp prick. Initially this was a shock, but he carried on cuddling me so I soon forgot it. My mother told me he was protecting me from possible problems but I did not understand. All I knew was that I was free to go out and about with Helen and my mother.

The vet ran 'puppy classes' at which we learnt to meet other dogs and which were great fun.

Helen took me out in her car to introduce me to the noises of traffic. Obviously, we had grown up with the background of noise from the countryside so my first visit to a town was not as frightening as it might have been. Helen took me with her when she went shopping in the village and called into the village pub so that I could get used to the noise of being in the company of a lot more men than I would normally meet.

One of the benefits of living with Helen was that I got used to the noise of television, phones, Hoovers, washing machines, dishwashers and other household equipment. We also walked through the woods near her home, where I was able to meet other dogs, most of whom were only too pleased to say hello and have a brief chat.

Frightened humans

But I was very puzzled by some owners who, as soon as they saw me, or any other dog, would put their dog on a lead and hold it tight so that they had no chance of talking to me. I could not understand it. Dogs which, when they were first approaching me, were wagging their tails and dying to be friendly, suddenly became snarling monsters.

If a dog was left to its own devices, he, or she, would meet me with the normal doggie politeness. We could mutually agree on our respective pecking orders. But, if a dog is being held tightly on a short lead, he or she will become so fearful that they respond, out of fear, in an aggressive way. What a pity. The dogs get themselves upset, the owners get themselves upset, and I miss the opportunity of having a nice friendly chat; particularly galling if the other dog is a handsome young collie!

I have certainly found, to my cost, that there is the occasional dog who is bad tempered, but even if we have the odd swearing session at each other and tell each other to 'get lost', the normal doggie processes of establishing a pecking order will fall into place, and it is a pity that some owners react too quickly and often cause a fight, which, had we been left to our own devices, would have been avoided.

Knowing how to behave

I was very pleased to stay with my mother and Helen because they were teaching me all the skills I needed to socialise with dogs, people, and the environment in which I would live. When I was about to leave to join my new family, the vet came to see Helen and to say goodbye to me. I heard him say to Helen that it was a pity that more owners didn't leave their dogs to have Helen's training, as both the owners and their dogs would be much happier, as I was.

While I was sorry to lose contact with Helen, her children and with my mother, I was keen to start my life with my new owners.

Chapter Eleven

My new life

Eventually the time came for me to leave my mother, Helen and her three lovely girls, who started to cry. I had mixed feelings. In one way I did not want to leave, but in another I was keen to meet my new owners and start my new life. The couple who came to collect me were the couple who had taken me to their home to see if I would settle down. This made me very happy, particularly when my new 'mum' took me to their car and settled me down in her lap while my new 'dad' ruffled my head in greeting.

When we arrived at their home, it seemed very nice and was close to the woods, which became my favourite source of walks. Once we got out of the car, my new dad took me into the garden and told me to 'be clean'. I wasn't sure what that meant, but I did need to go to the toilet and was told I was a good girl. I soon learnt when I needed the toilet I had to 'be clean' and when I did so I was 'a good girl'. Similarly when I needed to relieve myself I was told to 'do a big job' and when I did so, I was also praised as a good girl.

Once my new dad had gone through these commands a few times I knew what to do without being told.

Going to work

When, as a young puppy, I first joined my new owners, I found that they were 'working' and had an office in nearly Dartington. So, on my first day in my new home, I found myself going out to the car, being lifted onto Mum's lap for a cuddle, and going off to work. It was all a bit strange.

While Helen had worked hard to socialise me and make me familiar with human activities, I had never been into an office. Initially, I kept close to Mum or Dad but gradually, I began to explore the offices, get to know the various members of staff, and to enjoy the whole atmosphere. I had a cuddle on my mum's lap when going and returning to work, had a little walk around the office grounds when we arrived, was taken out for another walk mid-morning, and walked up to the Cot for lunch.

The office was a constant hive of activity with people coming and going. One afternoon a month, they'd close down the office, and every member of staff went over for a meeting in Dartington Hall. I went as well. It was very interesting, I didn't really understand what they were doing or saying but I could see that each member of staff or each little group of people would stand up and talk about how they were helping the company to succeed.

We had a lovely old boy called Alf, whom I used to keep company sometimes as he got the letters and parcels ready for posting. When it was his turn to speak at one of these monthly meetings, he had carefully analysed everything he was doing, and apparently pointed out ways in which they could save a lot of money. Everyone gave him a clap for his ideas. I couldn't clap, but I went over and gave him a friendly lick which he seemed to appreciate.

Retirement

Eventually, Dad and Mum stopped going to the office. I

didn't really understand it, but apparently they had 'sold' their business. I am still not sure what this meant, but what it did mean was that we spent more time at home.

Pack member

In short, I was a member of a nice little pack with my dad as the leader, my mum as the partner, and me as the junior member. I knew where I stood. They loved and respected me and often told their friends what a good dog I was. I loved and respected them. I was very fortunate to live in such a lovely 'pack'.

Exercise

My sense of well-being was enhanced by being given plenty of exercise. Let me just describe my normal routine.

First thing in the morning, as soon as Dad got up, we would go for our first walk of the day. We live near woods and we would go up to the gate at the end of the woods and back again. We didn't just plod along; our walks were turned into fun. There were paths made by other animals, foxes, badgers and occasionally deer, so Dad would send me down the one side of the lane, or up the other to investigate. There was one place in the path were there was quite a high hill to one side and quite a steep drop on the other. I would play 'king of the castle' (not sure what that meant) by Dad sending me up to the top of the hill and down the other. What mattered to me was that we were together, were having fun and benefiting from the walk together. We would always give each other a smile in the process.

After breakfast, I get a brief walk in the woods.

Mid-morning, invariably we'd go up into the woods again for a short walk.

After lunch, we used to have another major walk through the woods.

After tea, another short 'comfort' break-style walk.

After dinner, the third major walk of the day, sometimes with Mum keeping us company.

Bedtime walk, this was when we normally walked down the lane and as nights became darker the lane was lit.

Outings

We had quite a few shopping trips and while Mum went shopping, Dad would often give me a short walk.

Sunday was a real day out when we would either go up onto Dartmoor where Mum and Dad knew a lot of lovely walks. Again, these were turned into a game by Dad telling me to 'go round' a clump of bracken, or round a group of trees.

Other times we would go down onto the coast. There was a walk we enjoyed at Slapton, where I pretended to be a 'gazelle' by jumping the various clumps of bracken and other plants. Another favourite walk was Gara Rock, which I found frustrating because when we got to the hotel at the top of the beach, they would want to stop for a morning coffee and to read the papers. However, we would eventually get started and walk down to the beach where I would have a lovely time chasing the waves until summoned to resume the walk up to Prawle Point from which we would then return. I would take the chance of nipping down onto the beach again, for another run in the sea before catching them up over lunch at the hotel. It was a really lovely outing.

The walks I like best are when Dad and Mum go out together. I really feel part of the family. As they are getting ready, I shepherd them into order and keep returning to them to stress that we are a very tight pack.

Sundry outings

Whenever Dad works in the study, other little outings arise. He may have to nip down to the shop for Mum, or go down to the post office, or take and collect work from his secretary, which is sent across to Dartmouth where she lives. Any time there is any form of outing, I go with him. For me there is a little run up to the edge of the woods whilst he gets the car. Invariably when he leaves the car outside the post office he will leave the back open so I can watch the world go by and obviously, when we return, there is the chance of another quick burst into the edge of the woods as he collects his papers and walks back to the house.

Gardening!

Whenever Dad works in the garden, I am with him, helping when I can, or him giving me a silly game like being sent to fetch the 'blooming thing'. I have never succeeded in catching and fetching the 'blooming thing', but I keep on hurtling into the adjoining woods to see whatever it is! However, I like to help whenever I can. Once, Dad was trimming the branches of a tree, which fell down in an untidy heap, so I decided to take hold of each branch and move them into a tidy heap. I got a cuddle for my efforts. Similarly when Dad was trimming the edges of the lawn, I would take the cuttings away.

Company

*Company is vital for the health and
happiness of every dog.*

I have been lucky. I have had a life of constant company. In fact, the number of times that I have been left by myself could be counted on the fingers of my dad's hands. They were the occasions when it was extremely hot, or, extremely cold.

When we were at home, I had the choice of keeping my dad company in his study, or watching my mum wherever she was working in the house. If Dad was working out in the garden, I would be out there with him. In the evening, we would all sit down in the lounge together, and at night we would go up to bed where I had a nice bed of rugs on the floor next to Mum's side of the bed.

Whenever they went out in the car, I went with them.

'My' car

Whenever they went to change their car, I would go with them. I found it very exciting to go into the car dealership showrooms. When they opened the doors to look at the front and back seats of the car, I was there, having a good look myself, and a good sniff. But, the most important part of the visit was to look at the boot. We always had an estate car, so the most crucial issue for me was the size of the boot. On command, I would jump up into the boot and have a good wander around to see how big and comfortable it was, and to what extent the size of the seats allowed me to have a good view, or for one of the seats to go forward to give me an even better view. We once looked at a car where the back door sloped so steeply, that it severely limited the amount of room available to me. Once this was realised, the inspection was cancelled abruptly and we left to look at a car with more boot space.

Naturally, when we went out on a test drive, I was in the back and, quite obviously, Dad and Mum took particular note of how comfortable I would be. So, I had a crucial role in deciding which new car they would buy.

Fitting out 'my' car

When we got the new car home the first thing my dad did was to buy a four-inch deep piece of foam cut to the precise size of the boot area. He also bought a piece of good quality carpet, which, again, was cut to the exact size of the boot. On top of the carpet would be some loose rugs to make a very comfortable area should I wish to lie down. When I was younger, I seldom lay down, but wiggled my bottom into the corner of the boot, so that I was well balanced, and could watch the view as we went by. In fact, even on the long 500-mile drive to our holiday home in Ireland, I would be sitting, alert, watching the scenery as we went by.

Dad's illness

On my first visit to Ireland with them as a young girl, my dad had a heart attack. An ambulance was called to rush him on the 50-mile journey to Galway. Helped by some wonderful neighbours, my mum had to shut down the house and organise some supplies for me, and some clothes for herself, and charge after the ambulance. She felt very sorry for me as the car rocked from side to side on the twisting and bumpy roads; although I was quite well balanced in my usual corner. However, she started a game of pointing out the sheep and the cows we passed. I thought it was a good game, and would give a quick bark to confirm that I had seen them. Obviously, as a sheepdog, I was very interested in watching the sheep we passed, and, since sheepdogs are often used to fetch cows in for milking, I was equally interested in cows.

Returning to the subject of 'my' car, an important issue when we were deciding which car to buy was whether or not it had a convenient compartment for a large bottle of water, space for my bowl, and space for a towel. This meant that I could always be given a bowl of water when we either stopped on a journey, if I was left while they went shopping, when we were leaving for a walk, or returning at the end of the walk.

Without wishing to offend my dad's friends in the motor industry, any car is only a steel or aluminium 'box'. In summer, it can quickly become incredibly hot. Dad and Mum's concern was always to ensure that I would not get too hot. My bowl of water would always be available, the air conditioning in the car would always be on, and where relevant, the windows would be open. Great care was taken to ensure that if I was left, the car was left in the shade.

90

When we were going into the Eden Project, my dad asked one of the marshals where the best shady area was. He was told that there was a special area for dogs, to which we were directed. The Eden Project had a specially-built row of open garages, obviously carefully chosen with their backs to the sun and their sides either to the west or to the east, so that they were protected against the sun as it moved from east to west. My dad, mum and me, all thought it was really fantastic for the Eden Project to look after the increasingly-important number of dog owners who have their dogs with them when they are on holiday. Given the increasing number of dog owners who like to take their dogs with them, I heard Mum and Dad talking to each other and wishing more holiday resorts were equally understanding.

Saunton Sands

Talking of holidays, we once had a holiday in North Devon driving along the coast. One day, we stopped at a place with lovely sand dunes going down to an equally lovely beach. Dad and I got out of the car (Mum wanted to stay in the shade) and charged down the dunes to the sea. I had a lovely run, chasing the waves, and thoroughly enjoyed myself. But, when we went back to climb up the dunes we found it very hard work. It was quite a way back up to our car and the dunes were soft and very hot. I could only go a few yards before my feet were burning. I gave 'the eye' look to Dad, who realised that I had a problem. So, he came over and lifted me into his arms, and struggled with me up the dunes. It was hard work for him, fortunately there were the odd patches of grass, which were not quite as hot as the sand and so he could put me down to have a rest. By the time we got back to the car, Dad was exhausted and my feet were still hot. So, he put me back in the boot of the car, got out my water bowl, and put each foot in turn into the deep bowl. He did each foot four times to try to make sure that all the heat went from my paws. It was a great relief that the back of the car was so well equipped.

Cars can be cold

Rightly, there are many notices warning dog owners that cars can get very hot in summer, and can be dangerous to dogs if they are in the car too long in the heat. However, I never see any warnings that cars can also be very cold in winter. They may not be dangerous, but they can certainly be uncomfortable. In winter, a thick sheepskin rug is put into my boot area. This keeps my tummy nice and warm. Also, there is a thick woolly jacket in a corner of the boot which my dad or mum will put on me whenever necessary. They make sure that I am always warm and comfortable in winter, or cool and comfortable in summer.

Going out

My dad and mum used to go to the theatre in Plymouth, which was some way from our home, and I always went with them. First, I had their company for the hour or so it took to get to Plymouth and, again, I had their company on the return journey.

When we got to Plymouth, we always stopped near a park in which I could have a run and then parked in the multi-story car park behind the theatre. This was so well lit that the heat from the lamps kept the cold at bay and, invariably, my dad would nip out during the interval to give me another short walk.

So from my point of view, it was an outing I enjoyed far more than I would have done had I been left at home by myself.

If they went to the cinema in nearby Paignton, they would call in to leave me with one of their friends, Mary. The only problem was that Mary's cat seemed to fancy me and would want to cuddle up against me. As I got a bit older and needed more care, my friend Dorie would be asked to keep me company and to let me out for a brief walk when necessary.

Hotels

Dad organises three meetings a year for the Automotive Fellowship of which he is Chairman. They are held at the Danesfield House Hotel and Spa in Buckinghamshire, which has lovely grounds where I have had some marvellous walks. When we arrive, I lead the porter up to our room. The hotel staff are always very friendly to me, and invariably say hello or give me a pat whenever they see me. Obviously, Dad is busy at his meeting, and Mum likes to go off to Marlow for shopping, so I go to the conference. I'm not quite sure what it's all about but I enjoy the atmosphere and the greetings I get from the members present.

However, my dad used to give me a few exercises and games whenever he had the chance. One exercise involved me jumping through his arms. When the hotel staff saw this they started to ask me to jump through their arms. At subsequent meetings Dad and I made sure we could not be seen!

Friends

Dad and Mum have lots of friends and whenever they go to see them I go with them. I am always welcomed warmly and go with them on their walks, or lie down quietly if they are talking with each other.

Being polite, I always give everyone a friendly greeting when I meet them and when we leave.

Their friend Diedre in Ireland once had a party for some 50 people. I went with Dad and Mum and once I had had a polite greeting with Diedre, I hid under a chair. Nobody realised I was there until I emerged when it was time to go home.

Ireland

For the month of May and the month of September we go to our bungalow on the far west coast of Connemara in Ireland. It is over 200 miles from Devon to Fishguard, over on the ferry, an overnight stay at Cedar Lodge, and then a 225-mile journey across Ireland to Connemara and Clifden.

When I was young, I used to sit with my bottom in the corner of the boot, and watch the world go by with great interest, pointing out the cows and sheep we passed. Later in life, I must admit I spent more time lying down with just the occasional look out to see where we were.

Connemara is beautiful with lots of relatively deserted beaches and lovely walks, usually alongside a river or a lake. From our bungalow, we can walk down to Eyrephort beach where Mum and her friends like to swim. While I am busy chasing the waves, I keep an eye on Mum to be sure she does not swim out too far. If she does, I'll swim out and swim in front of her to make her turn back. I prefer her to swim along the beach rather than out to sea.

There's the lovely island of Omey connected by causeway, and the equally interesting island of Innisboffin. One particularly enjoyable walk is around the lake at Ballynahinch. I hear the humans saying that it was the home of the founder of the RSPCA. I have enough problems trying to understand their words so I can't really understand what this means. Possibly my favourite beach is Dog's Bay. I thoroughly enjoy running on the long stretch of beach with its interesting selection of waves.

Staying with friends

From time to time, I get worried by my mum packing suitcases. Are we going away together, or, horrible thought, are they going away by themselves. I get myself really tense, and when I was younger, used to feel almost sick with worry. Most times I went with them, to my great relief. But, sometimes they disappeared for a week or two, or three, usually when the word 'holiday' had been mentioned. I hated hearing the word holiday. As I got older, I became more relaxed, since I learned that I would always be left with one of my friends; sometimes with their son's dog. More often though, it was with my friend Wrinkles. But, just as we dogs can sense the imminent departure of our owners, so, too, can we sense their return. I'm really a bit rude, I don't wait to say goodbye. As soon as possible, I charge out and sit in my car keen to get back home.

Knowing how to behave

I am lucky, I have a very interesting life keeping my mum and dad company, going to visit their friends, and taking part in all their various activities. As I have indicated, I am accepted everywhere we go because *I know how to behave,* but so many dogs have a boring life either because their owners cannot be bothered to teach them how to behave, or, they have a very stupid idea that it is 'unkind' to expect a dog to go through the process of being trained.

As a very basic example, one day Mum had been shopping in the supermarket. She asked Dad to meet her to collect the shopping from her, and take the car while she went on to other shops. Going back to the car involved going down a circular staircase. Dad got himself into something of a tangle with the shopping. So, he very quietly told me to 'sit–stay' while he sorted himself out. While he did so, and while I waited patiently, another man passed us and said, 'I wish my dog would do that!' Fancy having a dog that will not do the basics of sitting down and waiting for its owner! I had had a nice little walk in the company of my dad and the stimulation of learning how to go up and down a circular flight of stairs. The other man's dog, at best had been left in the car, but, more likely, had been left without company at home, because he had not been taught how to behave.

Dogs need company and—collies in particular—need plenty of exercise. But, while we love our owners, we are dogs, we are pack animals, and we like meeting other dogs. Indeed, we need the friendship of other dogs. Again, I am lucky, I have many friends in the dog world and I'll just tell you about them to make my point.

Chapter Twelve

The friendship of other dogs

Hamlet

When I was a few months old, a marvellous being came into my life. I fell head-over-heels in love straight away. His name was Hamlet, though his friends called him Hammy. He was a black and white English pointer, standing over 30-inches high at his shoulders, with lovely long legs to match. His handsome black head, with its slightly upturned nose, gave me the quivers.

Hammy belonged to my owners' son, David, and his wife, Jacky, so we were able to meet on a regular basis throughout the years when either they came down to stay with us, or we went to them. Sometimes he used to come to stay with me while his owners went away on holiday and, equally, I have been to stay with him when mine have been away.

When we first met, I was barely a third of the height of one of his legs. Even when I was virtually fully grown, I had to race full-out to keep pace with his long, lolloping stride. My mother had told me that collies should always keep behind their master's heels. As a pointer, Hammy was bred to quarter the ground ahead of his master, seeking to

97

'point out' game. It was much more fun to join him so I soon forgot my mother's lessons.

I was never sure whether it was sheer naughtiness, or whether Hammy just got carried away by all the exciting scents. This used to worry me since all my breeding has been geared to keeping in eye contact with my master. So if Hammy disappeared, I would return to Dad for instructions, who would say, 'Fetch Hammy', and I would follow up his scent until I found him and then persuade him to chase me back to Dad and Mum. It was really exhilarating to race back together through the fields and lanes to where they were.

When we were in the house together we would have many a fine old game. Sometimes we played 'tug of war' with an old shirt of Dad's; other times we would have a mock fight, when I would have to stand on my hind legs to be better able to box his ears.

Hammy had a good life. He always went to the office with David and Jacky, so he had company all day long. They may not have had time for walks during the week but, every weekend they went for long walks through the woods. Once, on the snow covered Malvern Hills in winter, he had a lucky escape. He was running so fast he started to toboggan down the hillside as a car edged its way up the lane. Hamlet shot between the nearside wheels under the car and emerged beyond the offside wheels without a scratch. He was a great character in my life.

When he was 12 years old, Hamlet seemed to be failing fast but two things happened to give him a new lease of life. First, David and Jacky put him on a course of 'Devil's Claw', which seemed to offset the impact of arthritis and give him back his freedom of movement.

Second, they bought another, even bigger, pointer they called Macbeth; obviously shortened to Mac. Initially I felt sorry for Hammy because – understandably – Mac wanted to play continuously; even pulling Hammy around by his collar. But it gave Hammy a new lease of life, and he became much more outgoing and sprightly.

Sadly, when he was 14, which, I gather, is a good age for a pointer, he seemed to age rapidly and David and Jacky had to take the terrible decision that it was kinder for him to be put to sleep. As my 'first love', he will always be in my thoughts.

Macbeth

Mac is certainly a lovely dog, perhaps even more intelligent and handsome, and certainly far more obedient. Initially Mac was far too precocious for my liking. He seemed to expect to walk straight into a close relationship. I had to keep putting him in his place for taking liberties. Still, it's hard for a girl to resist such a handsome young dog, so I have begun to play with him, and better still, to race him up our lane. In fact, it's quite flattering to have such a handsome young 'toy boy' as my friend!

Judy

Mum's friend, Millie, had a blue roan spaniel called Judy, who virtually became an elder sister to me as we visited each other's homes. I used to delight in finding her squeaky toys and teasing her by parading around in front of her with them in my mouth. She did her best to get them back. It was a harmless enough game.

Coba

Another friend, who was virtually a second mum to me when I was young, was Coba the black Labrador. She used to live next door so we often met, and sometimes went for walks together. She taught me how to sniff out the fir cones and deposit them at Dad's feet, with the clear implication that he should throw them for me to retrieve.

Wrinkles

Wrinkles (what a name for a self-respecting dog!) belongs to Mum's best friend, Sally. At first, I was not sure I would like him. He was so dominant, even to his owners. If they did not feed him on time, he would bark to let them know of his displeasure—but, after a slow start, we became the best of friends and were pleased to spend time together. He, like me, loved the waves. When we were on holiday together once in Ireland, he made a noble attempt to chase me as I chased the waves; though with his short legs, there was no way he could catch me at full speed. He could be a bit cheeky. When his owners went away, he would come to stay and he would take over my position on the settee. Still, as friends, what did it matter? I certainly wish he was still around.

Sadly he developed an enlarged heart and kidney problems, and eventually died at the ripe old age of 18. He had a good life, and I still miss him.

Gypsy

One of my friends in Ireland is a lovely little bitch called Gypsy.

When I first started talking to her, she told me that she had had a very disrupted life when she was young and had been passed from one person to another. She had lost track of who and where they were, and why they had given her away.

Eventually, she had been given to a lovely lady called Emer who, Gypsy decided, was the human for her.

Emer was a solicitor who lived above the office so Gypsy appointed herself as Head Receptionist. She sat on the mat inside the front door and was the first person clients met when they came into the office. Gypsy started charging a fee for being allowed to enter the office, which was either a friendly rub of her ears, or a tummy rub for which she would turn over on her back. Clients who did not particularly like dogs and tended to ignore her merited a bark or two of disapproval from Gypsy.

Like me, Gypsy went everywhere with her owner. Indeed, when Emer and Gypsy walked down the town, more people would say hello to Gypsy than they did to Emer!

Gypsy told me that she particularly loved going to their holiday home on the island of Innisturk just off the coast. They went over on an old-fashioned Irish currach, which could sometimes be rather bumpy in bad weather. As soon as Gypsy got near enough, she would jump out of the currach and swim to the beach to start her favourite sport of chasing rabbits, with the occasional rest to cool off in the waves at the edge of the beach.

Gypsy told me that on one trip to the island, they had two of Emer's friends with them, one of whom, Kate O'Toole, had a very young Boston terrier pup with big brown eyes.

Gypsy had got used to the fact that the seagulls would hover over the stern of any fishing boats, so initially she took no notice of seagulls. She then realised they were hovering over their currach and gazing intently at the Boston terrier, which was young enough, and small enough, for them to dive down and take away as food.

Initially, she tried to warn her owner, Emer, by barking at her but Emer was busy steering the boat and did not get the message. Eventually, Kate realised that her puppy was the target, and held it close to her. When they got to the island, Emer gave Gypsy a really good cuddle by way of appreciation.

Gypsy thoroughly enjoyed her life with Emer in that she had the involvement of the people coming into and out of the office, she went for regular walks on the island with Emer, and travelled in the car with her on many of her journeys.

I always thoroughly enjoyed meeting up with Gypsy; particularly when we went to the island. She was always great fun, always friendly, and always affectionate to everyone she met. As a result, two or three of Emer's clients, who had never previously owned a dog, decided to get one.

Sadly, Gypsy died on the 8th August 2006 aged approximately 15, and is buried in her garden beside the sea. But, while Emer told my mum and dad that she was very sad at losing Gypsy, she would always have a special place in her heart, the fun, companionship and love she had had from Gypsy was such that Emer would buy a replacement dog in memory of her beloved pet.

Pandy

My friend Pandy was a real 'shaggy dog'. His pack leader was called Brian who, with his father Paul, ran the Abbeyglen Hotel, in Clifden, Galway. Hence, Pandy had the interest of a regular flow of guests into and out of the hotel, in addition to the inevitable visits of trades people. So, whenever we (my dad, mum and me) went to Abbeyglen, perhaps for a coffee or a meal, I would invariably meet up with Pandy and have a good chat with him.

His owner, Brian, ran regular 'safaris' to the other small islands off the coast, starting with a very interesting island called Innisboffin, which I always enjoyed going to; though I didn't particularly enjoy the journey over in the rather bumpy mail boat. Brian always had a crowd of people together with a local archaeologist on these trips and served a marvellous luncheon in a very interesting cave. Walkers held out their hands for a slice of smoked salmon, and then waited for a squirt of lemon juice. I think they found it rather fun.

Pandy and I enjoyed being among the crowd, but we particularly enjoyed being by ourselves, and while the archaeologist told people about the history of the island, Pandy and I had a good chat and a good run. On one corner of the island, my dad and mum liked to watch the seals, and the occasional whale, but I was more interested in the rather beautiful beach around the corner.

I was sad to learn, not long ago, that despite the best efforts of the local vet, Pandy had died, but he had certainly had a very fulfilling life.

Acquaintances

Apart from these very definite friends, there is a regular flow of other dogs up and down our lane to whom I say hello in a friendly manner as we pass each other. Some are friendlier than others, depending on the attitude of their owners who, so often, don't seem to want their dog to have the chance to talk. Sad.

There are two dogs in particular that I am always thrilled to meet and to have the chance to flirt with them.

Monty

One is called Monty, a smooth-haired retriever. He is a great bundle of fun, full of energy and enthusiasm. When we meet he bounds up to me full of vim and vigour. Though he doesn't spend much time taking, he really lifts my spirits.

Gyp

For some time now my real heart-throb is a good looking male called Gyp. He is a slim, tall lurcher with lovely long legs. We always have a good flirt when we meet. I think my dad must realise how I feel. If ever he sees Gyp in the lane when we are going out or returning from a trip in the car, Dad will stop and lift me out so we can maintain our flirtation. It's great fun.

Conclusion

In a nutshell, we dogs like the company of other dogs. There may be the occasional problem dog, but if we are left alone to establish our pecking order we will part in friendship.

Chapter Thirteen

Really enjoy your dog

Important to you and your dog

As I understand it, life is all too short for humans. If this is the case, it is even shorter for us dogs. It is important, therefore, not only that humans have a happy, fulfilling life with their dog, but that we dogs can equally have a happy, fulfilling life with our beloved owners. Let me quickly skim through the ways in which you can really enjoy your dog.

Think carefully

To avoid unhappiness, think through whether you should have a dog. Even committed dog lovers will accept that having a dog is a tie, which can get worse if you have to change your job, change where you live, or if any other circumstances, such as illness, disrupt your life.

Big dogs tend to have a shorter life span of ten years or so. Smaller dogs tend to live longer, my friend Wrinkles lived until he was 18. Do you really want to have between 10 and 18 years of commitment? Please think hard.

The right breed

Make sure you think very carefully when deciding on the type of dog you want. Talk to other dog owners, or consult your vet to make sure you choose the right breed of dog for you.

As one example, there is no way in which a diffident lady being dominated by her sister, should have bought my sister Hopeless. There is no way she could provide the leadership and the stimulation Hopeless needed. She ought to have bought a very small breed of dog, a miniature Dachshund for example, which she could easily lift up and carry.

I once knew a family with a very slightly-built young girl who was asking for a puppy. Again, the ideal dog for her would have been a relatively small breed, which she could lift up and carry and cuddle. Instead, her father went macho and bought a boxer, which was likely to grow into quite a big, strong, powerful dog. A young and slightly-built girl could not hope to control it. Even her mother found it difficult. Eventually the dog had to be given away.

Rescue dogs

Clearly, many dog lovers like to feel that the best thing they can do is to get a dog from a Rescue Centre. One advantage of so doing this is that the staff at the rescue centre will normally take a great deal of care to try to find the right people for the right dog. Some, like the Blue Cross, will actually give a potential customer a short training programme. But notwithstanding this, again it is a question of thinking very carefully.

Mothering your pup

If you decide to buy a puppy you will have the equivalent of a human three-year-old baby before your pup is fully house trained. That is to say, you will be buying a dog, ideally ten weeks old, who may not be fully puppy-trained until it is six months old.

I was lucky; both my dad and mum were very considerate. As soon as we arrived at my new home, I was taken out to a corner of the garden, to 'be clean'. Actually, by the time I arrived, I was desperate to 'spend a penny', and as I did so, I was told I was a 'good girl'. Thereafter I was taken out to the corner of the garden at regular intervals and told to 'be clean'. It got to the point where they merely had to open the back door, and I would trot off to 'be clean', or to have a 'big job'.

I was always taken out as late as possible before they went to bed, and Dad got up early in the morning to let me out. I did, in fact, have a pile of newspapers in the corner of the scullery if I needed it during the night, but I didn't need this very often. By getting up early, and going to bed late, and having regular visits to the garden in between, my dad and mum did not have any problems and I was fully house-trained quite quickly. But it can be an onerous period.

Will your dog have company?

Dogs cannot live without company. It is vital for the health and happiness of every dog.

I have been lucky. I always have the company of Dad or Mum or both. I went to work with them. I visited their business contacts with them. I went to the lectures that Dad runs. I went out with them to visit their friends. I have only been left alone of a few occasions, when it was exceptionally hot or exceptionally cold.

As I mentioned earlier, will your dog have a high level of company?

Leadership

Your dog is descended from wolves, who are pack animals with a pack leader. Similarly we dogs need a leader, so are you prepared to be your dog's 'leader'? If, by nature, you are a somewhat shy, retiring type who is always in the background at any activity, don't buy one of the bigger, more powerful dogs. If you show them that you are not prepared to act as their leader, they will decide that they will be the leader, which will cause incalculable problems and probably result in your having to get rid of the dog. Again, you will need a smaller breed of dog that you can control easily.

Understand your dog

Accept that we enjoy being touched; that we like to give and receive affection. Above all, recognise that our hearing is so sensitive that we cannot tolerate noise. When I was young, my dad used to whisper all his commands.

Earlier, as you may remember, I told the story of a man who was proudly showing off the fact that he had bought a 'silent' dog whistle to which his dog would respond. In effect, he had bought a whistle that was of a different sound frequency, which the dog could hear but the man could not. Then, when the dog came back to him he started to bellow at it. How stupid can a human get? At one moment you are accepting that the dog has very sensitive hearing; the next you are shouting loudly. Apart from the fact that this will be painful to your dog, he or she certainly won't be able to understand what you are saying.

Empathy

Make the effort to really understand your dog, watch him or her in action, note how they react to different circumstances and, in short, try to get into their minds.

My brother, Nosey, was bought by an owner who made absolutely no effort to understand him or his needs. You will remember that the man had an elderly mother who needed to have the television on loudly because she was deaf. This was torture to Nosey and he ran around the room trying to find some escape. The owner thought he was being naughty and smacked him to try to get him to lie down. Eventually, she gave up and, as a punishment, put him in the kitchen. For Nosey, this was a blessed relief.

We dogs try hard to understand our owners. We watch you carefully, and try to please you by anticipating your needs. But, we can't talk; all we can do is to use our body language, and in particular our eyes, to try to convey our needs.

For example, if I want help from my dad or mum, I will look very intently at them, or if they are asleep, I will lick their arm. Once I looked at my dad very intently, and went to stand by my water bowl, which, unusually, was empty. So, Dad filled my water bowl. On another occasion I had a bad tummy ache, so I ran to find Dad, looked at him intently, and then ran to the front door. Dad realised the problem, ran behind me and opened the door in time.

Exercise

Different dogs have different needs as far as exercise is concerned. But most need at least three reasonable walks a day. Hyperactive working dogs certainly need a high level of exercise and I typically have six walks a day, some quite long, others relatively short.

Friendship

As I mentioned in chapter 12, the friendship of other dogs is vital. You will remember that I gave you the details of some of my best friends. In addition, we dogs like to make contact with any other dogs we pass; something which some owners seem to resent.

Fulfilment

How far can you develop a relationship with your dog that helps to give him, or her, a sense of being a valued participant in all your activities?

Partly this means teaching your dog how to behave so that he or she can join in all your activities. But equally, so that he or she knows when to disappear under the table when necessary.

I always go everywhere with my dad and mum and fully enjoy my involvement with them, but I also know how to 'disappear'.

Obedience

Remember my earlier point that you have to be the leader of your pack even if it is only one dog. You need to set the theme, the atmosphere in which you want to interact with your dog. This does mean becoming a teacher, teaching your dog what you want, not by bullying, but by rewarding the behaviour that you find acceptable by giving a reward that your dog will enjoy, be it a titbit, playing with a ball, or just a cuddle.

Stability

Finally, to really enjoy your dog, you need to create an atmosphere of stability. You will remember my story of how my sister Happy had a very disrupted life and had six different owners. One was a real 'family from hell', with a large number of children and grandchildren, which created total mayhem. Eventually, Happy felt that she had to do something, and took charge. She attempted to round up the family in the normal collie way, but this resulted in all the different members of the family disappearing out of different doors, and even windows. The family demanded that Happy be killed but when the vet realised that the family had had no less than six dogs which had been put to sleep or deposited in different rescue homes, her life was saved. She ended up in a loving and stable relationship.

This was an extreme case, but can you provide stability?

Helpful summary

I hope you have found this a helpful summary of our

discussions and that it will help you to create a really enjoyable relationship with your dog.

Chapter Fourteen

My wonderful life

I have had a wonderful life.

My pack leaders

My pack leaders, my dad and my mum, have given me 16 years of unconditional love. If there was one thing of which I could be certain, the smiles they gave me, the cuddles, the quiet encouragement they gave me when teaching me how to behave, and the praise they gave me when I did something to please them, it was 16 years of totally unconditional love.

In turn, I gave them *my* unconditional love. I demonstrated my love by smiling at them, giving them a kiss, snuggling up against them to have a cuddle, and my instant obedience to every command they gave me, while often making sure that I did what they wanted me to do, without being told.

Their friends

Their friends were always very loving and understanding to me, which I tried to reciprocate, firstly by giving them a nice kiss when I arrived and a farewell kiss when I left; by enjoying their company on a walk, but, when necessary, disappearing out of sight.

My friends

As I explained in chapter 12, I have also been very lucky with the understanding friendship I have had with dogs I have known.

Hamlet, Macbeth and Wrinkles were really special, but I was lucky that my dad was so relaxed about my 'chatting up', not only the friends I mentioned earlier, but the dogs I met in the lane or when I was out and about.

Company

Virtually all my life, I had their company, and sometimes it was with my dad; sometimes it was with my mum, but ideally, most of the time it was with both of them. I shared their life totally; went to work with them; went with them to their friends; and shared in all their leisure activities.

The car was my second home so I kept them company on all their outings and journeys. When they went away on holiday, I went to stay with one of the dogs with whom I was friendly, and its owners.

Recently I heard my dad telling my mum that a lot of vets believe that dogs can watch over their master or mistress when they die.

It ties in with an experience I have had increasingly over the years. Every so often I sense that there is a shadowy figure of a black and white dog watching over me and my dad. It's odd, it's a rather shadowy impression I get but Dad has a picture of a black and white dog who, I gather, was once his constant companion who went everywhere with him, like me. He was called Herbert. Somehow, I always felt his presence was reassuring and I very much hope that I will be able to watch over my dad with him.

Ron Sewell – Daisy's dad

As a relatively young man, Ron Sewell founded, and for many years was Chairman of, the National Dog Owner's Association, committed to responsible dog ownership.

When he moved to Taunton, he founded and ran the Taunton Dog Training Club, and when he moved to Horsham, the Horsham Dog Training Club.

On returning to Totnes, he ran an annual summer school for dog trainers on how best to help owners to develop their dogs.

He has thus had an in-depth involvement with dogs and their owners.